HIGHLY SENSITIVE PERSON

THE SUPERPOWER OF ELEVATED FEELING

Subtitle: How To Use Your Enhanced Ability To Feel For Things Around You For Good And To Maintain Composure In The Face of Adversity and Social Anxiety

ANDREW CORNWELL

Table of Contents

PART I 15

Chapter 1: Why So Sensitive? 16

How To Tell If You're In The Camp... 17

What Makes People Overly Sensitive? 20

Negative Aspects Of Being A Highly Sensitive Person 21

    In The Workplace 21

    In Their Personal Lives 23

Chapter 2: Embrace Your Sensitivities 25

Benefits Of Being a Highly Sensitive Person......................... 25

    Having A Depth Of Experience And Feelings 26

    Self-Awareness... 26

    Intuitive Nurturing Skills 26

    A Knack For Forming Close relationships...................... 26

    Appreciating The Small Things In Life........................... 27

Why Highly Sensitive People Make Great Friends................ 27

Why Highly Sensitive People Make Great Employees 28

Chapter 3: Living As A Highly Sensitive Person 31

How To Overcome Your Sensitivities..................................... 31

Having Self-Esteem As A Highly Sensitive Person................ 33

    Accept Thoughts, Emotions, And Sensations As They Are 34

    Eliminate The Word "Should" From Your Vocabulary..................... 34

    Do Not Rely On Other People For Self-Esteem.............................. 34

    Forgive... 35

Take Stock Of Your Talents 35

Focusing On Jobs, You Are Good At.................................... 35

Caring Professions 36

Creative Endeavors 36

Clergy... 36

Academia.. 37

IT Professional 37

Dealing With Hyperarousal 37

Practice Mindfulness 38

Make Small Achievable Goals Towards Relaxation And Calmness 39

Positive Self-Talk 39

Investigate The Root Cause 40

PART II..42

Chapter 4: The Empath...43

How To Tell If You're An Empath 44

Problems That Empaths Deal With.................................... 45

Their Feelings Can Be Flipped Easily 46

Emotional Fatigue Is Real.. 46

Compassion Becomes A Burden.................................... 46

People Not Understanding Their Needs 47

Needing Time To Process Transitions............................. 47

It Can Be hard To Enjoy Yourself................................... 47

Get Taken Advantage Of 47

Saying "No" Is Difficult 47

What Creates An Empath... 48

Empaths And Toxic Relationships..................................... 50

The Victim 51

The Narcissist... 51

The Dominator... 51

The Judgmental One 51

The Innocent One 51

Chapter 5: The Empath Blessing...................................**53**

Empaths As Leaders... 53

Why Empaths Are Great Friends 54

Empaths Will Know When You're Not Well 55

They Know The Right Things To Say 55

They Can Protect You From Other People......................... 56

They Are Fun To Be Around.. 56

They Are Great Listeners 56

The Empath As A Spouse... 57

They Care About Making You Happy 57

They Make Amazing Parents 58

They Are Willing To Change For The Better 58

They Are More Tolerant And Understanding 58

They Want You To Be Yourself.. 58

The Love Is Passionate.. 58

They Are Great At Working Through Disagreements 59

They Hold You Accountable 59

Chapter 6: Protecting Yourself.....................................**60**

Protect Yourself Against Energy Vampires........................ 60

Realize They Exist... 61

Keep A Journal Of Your Gut Instincts.............................. 61

Have A Reality-Check Friend.. 61

Pat Yourself On The Back... 62

Put Yourself First... 62

Add "No" To Your Vocabulary 62

Prioritize Your Own Quality Time..................................... 63

Set Boundaries... 63

Harnessing Your Empath Power 64

Best Careers For An Empath.. 65

Nursing... 66

Artistic Careers 66

Psychologist Or Counselors... 66

Veterinarian.. 66

Musician.. 66

Teacher 67

Being Kind To An Empath.. 67

Chapter 1: Self-Care Is the Best Care 70

How Does Self-Care Work 71

How Does Self-Care Improve Self-Esteem and Self-Confidence?......... 72

Chapter 2: What Does Good Self-Care Look Like?................75

Good Self-Care Practices 75

Taking Responsibility for Your Happiness...................... 75

You Become Assertive With Others................................. 75

You Treat Yourself As You Would a Close Friend........... 75

You Are Not Afraid to Ask for What You Want............... 76

Your Life Is Set Around Your Own Values 76

Chapter 3: Demanding Your Own Self-Care.........................77

Setting Healthy Boundaries... 77

Identify and Name Your Limits 77

Stay Tuned Into Your Feelings 78

Don't Be Afraid of Being Direct 78

Give Yourself Permission to Set Boundaries 78

Consider Your Past and Present 79

Be Assertive 79

Start Small 80

Eliminating Toxicity and Not Caring About Losing Friends ... 80

Don't Expect People to Change 80

Establish and Maintain Boundaries 80

Don't Keep Falling for Crisis Situations 81

Focus on the Solution 81

Accept Your Own Difficulties and Weaknesses 81

They Won't Go Easily 82

Choose Your Battles Carefully 82

Surround Yourself With Healthy relationships 82

How to Focus on Self-Care 82

Pay Attention to Your Sleep 82

Take Care of Your Gut 83

Exercise and Physical Activity Is Essential 83

Consider a Mediterranean Diet 83

Take a Self-Care Trip 84

Get Outside 84

Bring a Pet Into Your Life 84

Get Yourself Organized 84

Cook Yourself Meals At Home 85

Read Regularly 85

Schedule Your Self-Care Time 85

Chapter 4: How to Be Happy Being Alone 86

Accept Some Alone Time 86

Do Not Compare Yourself to Others.................................. 86

Step Away From Social Media 86

Take a Break From Your Phone 87

Allow Time for Your Mind to Wander.............................. 87

Take Yourself on a Date.. 87

Exercise... 87

Take Advantage of the Perks of Being Alone.................... 88

Find a Creative Outlet... 88

Take Time to Self-Reflect 88

Make Plans for Your Future 88

Make Plans for Solo Outings 88

Chapter 1: Energy Healing- The Key to Holistic Health...................... 91

Chapter 2: Energy Healing and Overcoming Suffering 93

Energy and Grief/Trauma... 93

Energy and Mental Health 94

Daily Energy Regulation 95

Chapter 3: The Daily Energy Healing Journey................................... 97

Understanding Your Energy Field: Daily Energy Healing Meditation with Journaling (Week 5) 97

Protecting Your Energy Field: Daily Energy Healing Meditation with Journaling (Week 6)................................ 99

Healing Through Trapped Emotion Release: Daily Energy Healing Meditation with Journaling (Week 7) 100

Cultivating Self-Trust in your Healing Journey: Daily Energy Healing Meditation With Journaling (Week 8) 102

Mini Meditation Toolbox: 25 Quick and Easy Energy Restoration and Protection Meditations 104

PART V 121

Chapter 1: Anxiety, The Monster Within 122

How Anxiety Overshadows Everyday Lives 124

What is Anxiety? 125

Causes of Anxiety 125

Signs & Symptoms of Anxiety Disorders 127

Understanding Social Anxiety 128

Symptoms of Social Anxiety 128

Chapter 2: Acknowledging Your Anxiety 131

Common Anxiety Triggers 131

Getting to the Root Causes of Your Anxiety 132

Negative Self-Talk 132

Unrealistic Expectations 133

The "Should" Thoughts 133

Taking Things Too Personally 133

Pinpointing Your Anxiety 134

Chapter 3: Trauma and Anxiety 137

Childhood Trauma and Sensitivity to Anxiety 138

Common Anxiety Disorders Caused by Trauma 138

Chapter 4: Grabbing your life back from anxiety 140

Managing Your Emotions 140

Don't react right away 140

Find healthy outlets 141

Look at the bigger picture 141

Replace your thoughts 141

Forgive your triggers 142

Using the Power of Mini Habits 142

What Are Mini Habits?.. 143

What is *More* Essential than Your *Habits*?....................... 143

Benefits of Mini Habits.. 144

Chapter 5: Belittle anxiety with personal empowerment.................. 145

Smile.. 145

Focus on solutions, not problems.. 146

Notice the rise, not just the downfall 146

Just breathe 146

Fend off other's negativity 147

Switch the *"I have to"* mindset with *"I get to"* 147

Describe your life positively 148

Master rejection 148

Rethink challenges.. 149

Write in a gratitude journal... 149

Chapter 6: Everyday techniques to fend off anxiety 150

Visualization and Anxiety 150

Why You Should Be Using Visualization................................ 151

Aspects of Successful Visualization Practices....................... 154

Forms of Visualization for Anxiety....................................... 155

Meditation.. 155

Altered Memory Visualization.. 156

Receptive Visualization 157

Treasure Map 157

How to Design Your Own "Safe Space"................................. 158

Developing Anxiety Routines 161

Routines to Decrease Anxiety 162

The Importance of a Balanced Morning Routine 163

Benefits of a Morning Routine 163

Steps to Include in Your Morning Routine 164

Other Morning Methods to Relieve Anxiety 166

Chapter 7: Transforming Your anxiety for a better life....................**168**

Using Anxiety to Your Advantage 168

Redefining danger... 169

Channel your stress properly 169

Stop trying to do your best 169

Chapter 8: Battling anxiety like a true warrior............................... **171**

Spend time preparing 171

Learn to *manage* fear 171

Breathe.. 172

Don't keep things bottled up..................................... 173

Overpower that inner nagging voice 174

Think of the worst-case scenario.................................. 175

Reframe your mindset 175

Neuroplasticity 176

Get moving 176

Chapter 9: Rediscovering yourself after hurricane anxiety **179**

When were you the *happiest*? 179

What makes you *unhappy*?....................................... 179

Write!... 180

Learning to Love Yourself Again 180

Care about yourself as much as you care about others.................. 181

Maintain boundaries... 181

Do YOU? 182

PART I

Chapter 1: Why So Sensitive?

"For a highly sensitive person, a drizzle feels like a monsoon."

-Anonymous

When something out of the ordinary happens, and it is relatively minor, you may become a little surprised, sad, anxious, or happy, depending on what the situation is. Even though the event happened out of nowhere, it elicits a minor emotional response. This will be the case if your emotional reactions are that of a normal individual. However, if you are part of the subset of the population which is highly sensitive, then your response will be anything but minor.

Imagine going completely over the top with your feelings when something out of the ordinary happens in your life. If you go through a distraught situation, you become much more saddened than those around you. If a friend has something good happen to them, you will act more excited than they do. When someone is loud, you feel it to your core. If this sounds like you, then you might be a highly sensitive person.

Individuals who are highly sensitive display stronger reactivity to external and internal stimuli, whether emotional, physical, or social. They are thought to have deeper sensitivities at the central nervous system. It is estimated that about 15-20 percent of the population falls under this umbrella. Highly sensitive persons are believed to be much more disturbed by violence or tension. If they see something bad happen on the news, they will be distraught and might even be bothered by it the whole day. In contrast, someone who is not in their shoes will just think about it for a moment. On the flip side, if you make them happy, they will be exceptionally excited beyond control. It's how they are built.

This may not sound like a big deal to most. You have probably known several people who are overly emotional. However, this goes beyond just crying a little extra during a movie. If you were to go inside the mind of a highly sensitive person, what you are likely to experience would overwhelm you instantly. If you are living with this mindset, then you know exactly what I am talking about.

Despite what people may think, highly sensitive people are not dramatic for no reason. They often cannot help the way they react in certain situations. At least, not without becoming aware of it first. These individuals will often notice things much more acutely than other people do. This relates especially to the feelings of others. While most individuals will simply overlook the pain and suffering of someone else, a highly sensitive person will be more aware of their emotions. They may not know exactly what is wrong, but just that something is okay. They will pick up on the subtleties of body language, facial expressions, and tone of voice. Even if they don't know an individual, they will be in-tune with the vibes the person puts off. All sensitivity radars will be off the charts.

How To Tell If You're In The Camp

If you have always felt a little different than everybody else around you, then you might be dealing with a highly sensitive personality. Of course, there are many different attributes to consider before knowing for sure. The following are some of the signs of being in this camp. Once you understand whether you're a highly sensitive person or not, then we can proceed forward.

- You are extremely unsettled by cruelty or violence. While most people don't enjoy violence, a highly sensitive person will become extremely disturbed or physically ill by it, even if they don't see it personally.
- You are frequently emotionally exhausted because of how others feel. Essentially, other people and their feelings have a deep impact on you.
- Time crunches make you extremely anxious and overwhelmed. While approaching deadlines can make anyone's hair get raised, it is exponentially greater for a highly sensitive person.
- You enjoy going int solitude at the end of the day to reduce your stimulation levels.
- You are very jumpy and become frightened quickly.
- You are a very deep thinker. You often reflect on your life and experiences to process everything. You will also play events in your head over and over again.
- You seek to find answers to life's questions and wonder why things are the way they are.
- You are startled easily by sudden, loud noises.
- You have reduced pain tolerance.
- You have a rich inner world. You probably grew up with many imaginary friends and might still have them as an adult. You frequently go into a fantasy world.

- You are extremely upset by change, whether positive or negative. It can really throw you off.

- You are very sensitive to the environmental stimuli around you, like the birds chirping, sirens, new smells, or unusual sites. This is because all of your senses are heightened.

- When you're hungry, you become angry too.

- You hate conflict and disagreements. You want people to get along and not fight with each other. You definitely avoid confrontation if you can.

- You are very thin-skinned. You do not take criticism well, whether it is constructive or not.

- You're very conscientious of making mistakes. You're not perfect, but you try extremely hard to be.

- The beauty of your surroundings moves you deeply. Whether it is artwork, a rich scent, or a delicious looking meal, you are enthralled by all of it.

- You will compare yourself to others and often feel inferior as a result.

- You are very perceptive and insightful. You pick up on things that others don't.

If you have been dealing with the issue of being highly sensitive, then you have probably been looked down upon your whole life. People may have told you to toughen up, be less sensitive, or grow a backbone. Don't take any of these statements personally because these individuals did not know better. In fact, you may not have known better and thought there was something wrong with you. Well, as you read further, you will actually begin to understand your unique gifts.

What Makes People Overly Sensitive?

There are many factors to consider when deciding on why you are a highly sensitive person. If having these feelings is an anomaly for you, meaning it's not your normal personality, then it is probably a unique life event that is causing you to behave in this manner. For example, losing a loved one, having poor health, not eating properly, or getting a lack of sleep may contribute to feelings of over sensitivity. However, if you have always been this way, then it goes well-beyond life events. It is ingrained in you to be a highly sensitive person.

Children who were severely criticized, bullied, or went through some type of abuse or trauma can also end up being highly sensitive. Their psyches took a major hit while they were children, so they grew up to be unsure of themselves, which may have contributed to their over-sensitivity, as a result.

Your highly sensitive feelings are likely to have a genetic component to them. So, you might have been born this way as it was passed on through your genes. Also, environmental and social factors may be involved. If your parents, or those you grew up around, were highly sensitive people, then you might have picked up on their personality traits and acquired them as your own. Of course, you can also end up completely opposite from your parents and other influential people, so their attributes may not mean anything in relation to you.

Overall, a highly sensitive person is thought to have a brain that is wired differently, so it has a lower threshold for the environment. So, any type of stimulus will have an exponential effect on them. Many of these characteristics can be seen in babies, as some infants are much more emotional and sensitive to things like sound. This further suggests that people are born highly sensitive, rather than made. In the mid-1990s, husband and wife psychology duo, Arthur and Elaine Aron, coined the term "sensory-processing sensitivity," which is the official scientific phrase used to describe a highly sensitive person. Through their research, the husband and wife duo stated further that the nervous system of someone with sensory-processing sensitivity had variations in their nervous system that was different from others who did not display highly sensitive qualities.

Negative Aspects Of Being A Highly Sensitive Person

Being in the camp of high sensitivity can certainly have their advantages, which we will go over in the next chapter. For now, I will discuss the negative aspects of being a highly sensitive person. This personality trait can impact every area of your life, and if you are not careful, it can create a lot of pain and suffering in the long run. Unfortunately, people will take advantage of the kind qualities of a sensitive individual, and the results are not always pleasant.

In The Workplace
If you are like the majority of people in the world, then you probably spend much of your time in the workplace. Here, you will have regular interactions with your coworkers and those in upper management. While certain things in the workplace may be a slight struggle or annoyance for most individuals, a highly sensitive person may have their whole workflow and mood affected in a significant way. The following are certain obstacles that only a highly sensitive person would understand and contend within the workplace.

- A strong aroma in the office can completely throw off a highly sensitive person. These can be smells that come from different foods or from someone wearing a lot of perfume.

- Other sensory issues like bright colors or loud sounds in the workspace, can severely affect their focus and ability to do their job.

- Trying to complete last-minute deadlines without proper planning can cause a highly sensitive person to become overwhelmed quickly. This is definitely not when they do their best work.

- Criticism from a boss or employee can truly mess with a highly sensitive person's head. They may even react in an unorthodox fashion, like having a mental breakdown, crying excessively, or running out of the office. They often cannot help it as it is an instantaneous reaction.

- Highly sensitive people will have a hard time speaking up and asking for what they want or need. They hate rocking the boat and definitely don't want to upset anyone else. As a result, they are often overlooked for many opportunities.

- These individuals are often seen as weak and ineffectual, so people will walk all over them. The highly sensitive person will usually let them.

- They are usually overstressed, even if it's a normal workday with nothing unusual going on. Anything in their environment can make them feel this way. Remember that highly sensitive people are more prone to be affected by environmental stimuli.

- There will be constant comparison with coworkers, and the highly sensitive person will always feel like they come up short.

- Wearing professional clothes, like ties, high-heels, or various other things that are uncomfortable, are highly bothersome to you.

As a highly sensitive person, you must be aware of these unique traits and how they will make you react. Otherwise, your experience at work will become constant suffrage.

In Their Personal Lives

Highly sensitive people will also deal with others in their personal lives, both at home and in various relationships. Their personality traits will often not do them any favors in this aspect of their lives, either. As a highly sensitive person, you will have extremely emotional and sometimes hostile relationships with those close to you. The following are some issues you may run into.

- Highly sensitive people will sense when their friends and family are going through some issues. They will also allow these emotions to overwhelm them.
- If a highly sensitive person gets asked to do something, in most cases, they will say yes, no matter how busy their schedule is or what they have planned. Saying no is a true challenge.
- These individuals are their own worst critic and will be excessively hard on themselves for something, while easily forgiving someone else for the same issues.
- They are often poor with self-care because they are too busy worrying about others.
- They are more sensitive to trouble and conflict within a relationship. They will become stressed easily during a conflict.
- They will have a lot of self-doubt about their abilities, which will show in their personal relationships. They will usually be the ones to submit and compromise full.
- They will have a hard time asking their friends for anything.

- It will be very easy to hurt a highly sensitive person's feelings. Plus, they can be manipulated easily.

As you can see, a highly sensitive person will not have an easy time with their personal relationships. They will usually be the givers and never the takers. These qualities can wear down on them and create much emotional and psychological harm if not dealt with accordingly.

Now that we have a picture of what a highly sensitive person is, you probably have a pretty good idea if you are one or not. We will get into more detail about the positive qualities of this personality trait.

Chapter 2: Embrace Your Sensitivities

I know I was pretty hard on highly sensitive people in chapter one and did not paint them in the most positive light. It is hard to imagine that these individuals actually have positive qualities. However, just because a highly sensitive person has flaws and weaknesses does not mean they don't have significant strengths too. In this section, I will go over the reasons why being a highly sensitive person is a good thing and how people can start embracing this aspect of themselves.

Benefits Of Being a Highly Sensitive Person

There are actually many great qualities to being a highly sensitive person, and the world is lucky to have individuals like this. Sensitivity is falsely depicted as being undesirable, which you have probably noticed in your own life. I am here to tell you that it is not a negative trait to have. With all of the controversy surrounding it, the benefits are often overlooked. But, they cannot be ignored any longer.

Having A Depth Of Experience And Feelings

Experiencing the world with heightened emotions gives you a deeper meaning in everything around you. You learn to find joy in the smallest things, which means you have the ability to find good in every area of life. You learn to experience life in a totally different way as a highly sensitive person and notice beauty in the subtleties of life.

Self-Awareness

Self-awareness means having a strong sense of who you are and where you belong in the world. A highly sensitive person has a keen self-awareness. They are hyper tuned in to their emotions, and the reactions that follow them. While a highly sensitive person understands their high levels of emotional volatility, they eventually realize that other people do not process feelings in the same manner that they do. What throws their minds for a loop, will barely be a blip on the radar for someone else.

Intuitive Nurturing Skills

The highly sensitive person is naturally good at nurturing others. Because of their ability to feel deeply, they have a strong desire to bring happiness to other people. They have the instinct to care for others and will support them, so they feel loved and appreciated.

A Knack For Forming Close relationships

Highly sensitive people may take a while to open up to somebody, but once they do, they form strong bonds in the process. They will become the best companions a person can have. The reason highly sensitive people are choosy with making friends is because they can feel the energy of others around them. If the energies don't mesh, they know the relationships won't be a good fit.

Highly sensitive people are not interested in casual acquaintances, but in developing meaningful relationships. They want to be around individuals who make them feel comfortable.

Appreciating The Small Things In Life

Highly sensitive people are also highly sensitive to things that bring them joy. This means they can find joy in even the smallest things in life. If they are having a bad day, hearing a good song on the radio can completely change their mood.

Why Highly Sensitive People Make Great Friends

As we move through life, we meet and develop relationships with many different people. While we get along and also get to know these individuals well, how many of them truly become great friends? It is rare to find friends who understand us for who we are, leave us feeling warm and make us believe that we are important. A highly sensitive person is a friend who has all of these abilities. These individuals become the best kinds of friends because of the attributes they possess. The following are a few reasons why a highly sensitive person should be a sought-after relationship in your life.

- They are able to manage conflicts well because they have the ability to observe and quickly diffuse a situation. Plus, they have a keen eye for details and can often sense a conflict erupting before it starts.

- They highly understand the needs of others and will work hard to keep their friends happy, including you.

- They like to involve others and help them grow. Even when you make a mistake, they will help you learn from it and maintain your confidence.

- They are not stuck in their own worlds.

- They have a sense of purpose and want to make a difference in people's lives.

If you are a highly sensitive person, know that you can be a great and valuable friend to many people out there.

Why Highly Sensitive People Make Great Employees

While highly sensitive people can struggle in major ways in many work environments, they actually make great employees. The attributes they have make them reliable, hardworking, intuitive, and great team players. Rarely will they cause drama. In fact, they will do their best to avoid it.

Highly sensitive people are often undervalued in the workplace. They are not the most charismatic or outspoken people in the office. In fact, they are probably the ones you will hear from the least. Unfortunately, the soft skills they bring to the table do not get the same recognition as the stronger skills. This does not mean they are less valuable as employees, though. The following are some of the reasons highly sensitive people are a great addition to any company.

- They are the ones you can count on. They have the right attitude, will always show up, and will put in the effort needed to get the job done.
- They are careful decision-makers and will rarely take action hastily. As a result, the decisions they make are often the best possible under the circumstances at the moment.
- If they are in a positive environment, they will thrive beyond your imagination.
- They can be creative and, therefore, find the right solutions to problems.
- People often think that leaders have to be loud and brash. Actually, this is the opposite of what a leader should be. True leaders are intuitive, listen well, and inspire others. This is why a highly sensitive person actually makes a great leader.
- Highly sensitive people will focus on what benefits the team, rather than what benefits themselves.

If you are a highly sensitive person, know that your attributes are truly desired in the workplace, even if it doesn't seem that way.

Guess what? As a highly sensitive person, you are special and bring a unique gift to this world. Too many people are stuck in their own heads and have no concept or understanding of the world around them. You, on the other hand, can acknowledge the thoughts and feelings of other people. Because of your great attributes, you must stop believing that you are undesirable or weak. You are actually the strong one. The next chapter will discuss how you can start believing in yourself and the value that you bring to the world. You will become a better person overall.

Chapter 3: Living As A Highly Sensitive Person

The key to living a happy life as a highly sensitive person is to embrace the good qualities that you possess and showcase them to the world, while not allowing your flaws to control you. The bad part about highly sensitive people is that their oversensitivity gets the best of them, and often at the most inopportune times. The goal of this chapter will be to focus on controlling your emotions and allowing your unique gifts to shine through by using specific action steps to rewire your brain and way of thinking. Mindset shifts will be a major factor in managing your habits and sensitivities. Once you go through the practices and action steps I discuss here; you will truly be able to live your best life as a highly sensitive person.

The first step in the process is realizing who you are. In the previous two chapters, I detailed the positive and negative attributes of a highly sensitive person. In the end, while having this trait has extreme downsides, the positives outweigh the negatives. If you have come to realize that you are a highly sensitive person, then it's time to move on to the strategies and actions steps to manage your emotions.

How To Overcome Your Sensitivities

Just to be clear, you will never get rid of your sensitivities. They have always been a part of who and always will be. The objective is to manage these sensitivities, so you can overcome them. If they control you, they can become a major obstacle. The key is to use them to your advantage by controlling them. The following are some survival tips for highly sensitive people so that they don't become overwhelmed.

- Get plenty of sleep. Usually, 7-8 hours is recommended, but whatever it takes t make you feel well-rested. A lack of sleep will make you irritable, moody, less productive, and decrease your concentration. Proper sleep will help soothe your senses.

- Eat healthy food throughout the day. People dismiss how much of an effect diet has on your mood. But, if you eat foods high in cholesterol, saturated fats, and sugars, you will become tired, irritable, and overly sensitive to stimuli.

- A good pair of headphones can keep you from getting triggered with loud noises. You cannot control the noise, but you can manage how much it affects you.

- Plan time to decompress. Being on the go all the time will always keep you on heightened alert. This means you will continuously be in a frazzled state of mind. Taking time to decompress, preferably at night, can allow your nerves to calm down and no longer be affected by external stimuli. Whatever you can do to isolate yourself from the craziness of the world, do it.

- Give yourself the time and space to get things done. Highly sensitive people do not do well with a packed schedule, so avoid getting yourself in this position if you can help it.

- Limit your caffeine intake. Caffeine is a natural stimulant that will make you feel jittery if taken in excess. Highly sensitive people might be even more sensitive to caffeine. If you drink two cups of coffee a day, cut it down to one.

- Try to avoid excessively lighted areas if you can. In your home, keep your lights dim, as well.

- Get your errands done during the off-hours. This means going out opposite the average person's regular schedule. Get your shopping done during the week, go out with friends on weeknights, and go to the gym early in the morning. The goal here is to avoid huge crowds that can stir up your emotions.

- Get out in nature as much as possible and get away from the hustle-and-bustle of the city.

Even though you are born being highly sensitive, there are still many environmental factors that can trigger you to become more over the top. The survival tips above are meant to prevent overloading your hypersensitive senses. Many psychologists and research scientists have stated that a proper lifestyle may not change our genetics, but it can keep it from making our issues worse.

Having Self-Esteem As A Highly Sensitive Person

Te thing that highly sensitive people struggle with the most is their self-esteem, which is the value and worth they place on themselves. This is because they allow their environment, including the people, around them, to dictate their emotions. It is difficult for these individuals to break away from the feeling other people are having. As a highly sensitive person yourself, it's time for you to start realizing the importance of self-esteem and begin to recognize ways you can improve your own. It is time to stop thinking you are not good enough.

The following strategies will take a lot of practice, but once you start implementing them, you will notice major changes in your mindset.

Accept Thoughts, Emotions, And Sensations As They Are

All of these aspects are a part of you but do not define you. They are fleeting in nature and are changing from moment to moment. If you are feeling pain, whether emotional or physical, for a definitive moment, that does not mean you are weak. It is a sensation you are going through that will eventually pass. Instead of letting your thoughts and feeling control you, work on observing them objectively and then letting them go. Do not allow them to become attached to you.

Eliminate The Word "Should" From Your Vocabulary

When you use the word "should," it will elicit a sense of guilt inside of you. If you change it to "could," then you subconsciously open up your mind about what you could be doing and uses less judgment. Using the word "could" also showcases that there are many different options for us, and we are not required to stay on one path. Try it out:

"I should be going to the gym." Change it to, "I could be going to the gym." See the difference?

Do Not Rely On Other People For Self-Esteem

Unfortunately, as highly sensitive people, most of our self-worth is dependent on what other people think of us. You will never place true value on yourself if this is the mindset you will carry. The major problem is that when our outside source for self-esteem vanishes, then the opinion we have of ourselves plummets. We have to internalize our power to create our value and become the sole person who is in charge of it.

Forgive

We all have something in our past that we are not proud of. We must learn to forgive ourselves for the mistakes we made so we can move on. We need to apply the same compassion for ourselves that we tend to show other people. The next time you are hard on yourself, imagine one of your best friends standing in your position. Now, picture what you would tell this person if they made the same mistakes you did. If it's something favorable, then tell yourself the same thing. Stop being your worst critic.

Take Stock Of Your Talents

We tend to focus on our faults, and this severely lowers our self-esteem. We do not give ourselves enough credit by doing this. It is time to take stock of your talents and remember the gifts that you bring to the world. Identify what you are good at. If you are having a tough time coming up with something, then start small. Perhaps you are good at putting things away. This is a good start. As you come up with things, write them down and keep them to look at constantly. Another exercise you can do is write down what you think you're not good at and then crumble up that piece of paper and throw it away. Focus on your positive attributes.

Remember that these exercises will take a lot of consistency. Do not just quit after one day. When you begin incorporating these strategies into your daily life, you will see vast improvements with your mindset.

Focusing On Jobs, You Are Good At

I discussed in the previous chapter about highly sensitive people being model employees. This is still true. However, the goal is to make yourself as happy as possible, and this means avoiding things that will trigger your sensitivities. That being said, there are certain environments and job types where a highly sensitive person will fit in better and even thrive. If you can avoid the stress altogether, then why not do so? The following are the best career options for you if you are a highly sensitive person.

Caring Professions

Careers that require a lot of caring and compassion will be right up a highly sensitive person's alley. These jobs include things like nursing, medicine, counseling, therapy, and coaching. These fields will target a highly sensitive person's strength. Bear in mind that certain areas, like the emergency department or the ICU, may be challenging areas for you. Also, any busy environment will have a lot of different emotions that you will have to contend with. Good options in these fields may be things like home health nursing or individual counseling.

Creative Endeavors

Highly sensitive people are often very creative, so they will thrive in professions where they can show off their creativity. Some of these roles include graphic designer, writer, photographer, artist, or architect. Many creative jobs can be done on a freelance basis, which allows you to create your own schedule. This will be a major benefit to you as a highly sensitive person.

Clergy

If you have a spiritual side to you, then working as a clergy person may be right for you. Bear in mind, that depending on the denomination, you may have to follow strict rules. This may cause difficulty if you are a highly open-minded person. Of course, if you can get over the structure, then your intuition and sensitivity will be valued and accepted.

Academia

With academia, you get to spend a significant amount of time doing thoughtful and intensive research on a subject you have an interest in. In addition, you get to teach your extensive knowledge to students; as a highly sensitive person, you will thrive in your areas. In the end, you are doing meaningful work throughout your profession.

IT Professional

Coding is a major portion of IT and requires a lot of creativity to be successful. You will also need strong intuition and an eye for detail. These are all qualities that are possessed by highly sensitive people. As one of these individuals, software engineering or website development might be the perfect career paths for you.

When choosing a career to go into, you should focus on your strengths and what areas you will be compatible with. Consider your strengths as a highly sensitive person and determine what line of work fits you best.

Dealing With Hyperarousal

There will be times when you are in a state of hyperarousal, where you will be wired up and out of control, physically and mentally. In some cases, hyperarousal can be a defense mechanism, like with the fight-or-flight response. In these moments, being on high alert is a necessity. However, when the hyperarousal goes beyond defined moments, you will be dealing with many problems, including stress, anxiety, and overall diminished emotional and physical health. Yes, being in a state of constant arousal is detrimental to your physical health. Prolonged stress has led to many chronic illnesses, like heart disease, stroke, diabetes, and even some cancers. In addition, mental health disorders like depression are also a possibility.

When you are in the hyperarousal state, you will have an increased heart rate, faster breathing, quicker reflexes, perspiration, and heightened sensitivity to stimuli. So, when you hear a loud noise, you will immediately jump into action, or at least be ready to. Once again, short-term physiological responses like these are not dangerous. If you are consistently in this state, then we have a problem that must be addressed.

Hyperarousal needs to be dealt with quickly; otherwise, it will take over your life. This response is a symptom of another problem, so if you can figure out that problem is, then you can address it directly. The following are some action steps that will have a favorable response to being wired.

Practice Mindfulness

The purpose of this technique is to sit peacefully and consciously observe the chaos and frantic thoughts going on inside your mind without trying to change them, escape from them, or fight them off. Many therapists use this technique with their clients because it is effective in getting over feelings of panic. It also helps to reduce your hyperarousal symptoms.

Perform this technique for about 1-5 minutes at a time. Just sit quietly and focus on your feelings of discomfort, agitation, and anxiety. Concentrate very hard in this area. See if you can visualize these negative feelings and imagine holding them in your arms. A common practice that therapists have their clients do is picture the problems they are holding as being much bigger and worse. It may sound confusing, but it works well for their clients. It is likely because once they've imagined the issue being worse, the thing does not seem as major.

Make Small Achievable Goals Towards Relaxation And Calmness

I do mean to make these goals achievable by keeping them small. When you first start out, shoot for 30 seconds of pure relaxations. Once you achieve this milestone, then try for one minute, then two minutes, and so on. Eventually, you will be able to be in this state for several minutes with no problems. Just work your way up.

It does not matter what relaxation techniques you use, as long as you are in a state of physical relaxation and calmness. This can mean lying down in bed, sitting in a comfortable chair, or meditating. The choice is yours. From here, remain quiet and focus on a body part that feels tense. Now, take one breath in slowly over a few seconds, then hold it for a few seconds before letting it out slowly. As you release the breath, imagine the tension leaving that part of the body you focused on earlier. Truly visualize the tension dissipating like a cloud of smoke.

Evaluate yourself after this. Did your breathing and pulse rate decrease? Do you feel less tense and anxious? If so, then the practice was a success. Keep working on this step to make yourself better.

Positive Self-Talk

In the middle of frantic self-talk that is negative, interrupt yourself and begin saying some encouraging phrases. These include statements like, "You will get through this," or "You are strong and will overcome." This technique will trick your mind and shift it from positive to negative. As a result, you will slow down your pace. Once you do this often, it will become a habit.

Investigate The Root Cause

The above exercises are beneficial; however, you should also determine what the root cause of your hyperarousal is. If you can figure this out, then the risk of flareups in the future will go down. Some of the causes include anxiety, PTSD, excess caffeine, and drug or alcohol use. Once you've narrowed it down, then you can focus on more specific techniques to eliminate the root cause.

For example, Cognitive Behavioral Therapy, or CBT, can be an effective strategy from anxiety. The goal of CBT is to challenge your current thought patterns through talk therapy. The following are a few key steps to make CBT work for you.

- Identify what you are thinking by actually writing them down on something. This way, you can visualize them.
- Assess your thoughts and realize that they may not be true or accurate. We often think negative thoughts for so long that we automatically assume they identify us, and we never challenge them.
- Replace these harmful thoughts with more positive and encouraging ones. Write down all of these new thoughts, as well.

- Now, read these new thoughts to yourself over and over again. Do this until it becomes a habit for you to think of these thoughts, which could take days or weeks.

CBT is a strategy that works for many different disorders, and therapists use it often.

The bottom line to all of this is that you will always be a highly sensitive person. It is not something you can avoid, nor should you try to do so. Despite the challenges that may exist, being a highly sensitive person is still a unique gift that you should embrace every day. Learning the techniques to control your thoughts and emotions, and not allowing your environment to overwhelm, you will ensure that you live a happy and satisfying life. Your sensitivity and intuitiveness are a true gift for many people.

PART II

Chapter 4: The Empath

Imagine standing next to somebody on the street. You don't know them, nor have you have any type of communication with them. However, you can sense that this person is not doing well. They are sad and hurting on the inside. You don't understand why they have these feelings, but you know that they do because you can feel them within yourself too. This may sound like a far-fetched reality, but it's not. This is something that occurs when an individual is an empath.

Empathy means that you have the ability to sense and feel what someone is going through fully. This goes a step further than what we have already described in the first three chapters. While a highly sensitive person can understand and even relate to the emotions around them, an empath actually has the ability to feel those emotions within themselves. For example, if someone near an empath is sad and depressed, the empath will feel it inside of them as if they are standing in that person's shoes.

Dr. Judy Orloff, who is a professor of psychiatry at UCLA and a pioneer in the field of empathy, suggests that while highly sensitive people still have a barrier towards the stimulation in the environment, an empath has no filter, so absorbs everything around them like a sponge in a bowl of water. This makes it very hard for empaths to protect themselves and their emotions. They are also very sensitive sounds, strong personalities, and busy environments. They basically feel everything to a very high degree, and one of the reasons they become overwhelmed is because they cannot decipher or separate the emotions from their own. This means that as the emotions are coming in, like sadness, happiness, or anger, they have a hard time telling if they are feeling that way, or someone close to them is.

How To Tell If You're An Empath

There are many unique traits that empaths possess. The following are some of these qualities. If these sound familiar to you, then you may be an empath too.

- They are world-class nurturers and naturally giving. If you want someone by your side through thick and thin, then an empath is your person to go to.
- They are highly attuned to the environment around them, to the point that they feel everything down to their core. They might as well be standing inside of a person's body because they are feeling their emotions so closely.
- They are uncomfortable in large crowds because they are being inundated with all of the thoughts and feelings surrounding them, which can become very overwhelming and very exhausting.

- As a result of being uncomfortable in large crowds, empaths are often introverts. They usually prefer one-on-one interactions, rather than being in groups settings of any sort.

- Since it is draining for them to be around so many people, empaths need their alone time to help them recharge.

- They love nature as it nourishes and restores them. An empath would rather walk on a nice hiking trail than a city block.

- They have very finely tuned senses, so they are very sensitive to smells, noise, and excessive talking. If you touch an empath, don't be surprised if they jump a little bit.

- Since empaths can deeply feel the pain in others, they try very hard to relieve that pain for them, even if it's at their own expense.

The last person an empath thinks about is themselves. This is unfortunate because they are the ones who usually need the most care. While empaths have very appealing personalities on the surface, they often go through a lot of suffering because of the innate qualities they possess. The focus of this chapter will be the negative factors that come from having empathic traits.

Problems That Empaths Deal With

With all of the attributes that empaths have, they are bound to run into problems when dealing with the real world. While many people can separate themselves from others, it is nearly impossible for an empath to do the same. They are constantly sucked into the trials and tribulations of society, and as a result, are constantly dealing with significant emotional issues.

Empaths are often misunderstood. People who are not in their position cannot fathom what is going on in their minds. However, an empath is burdened with so many things that it becomes hard for their mind to cope with everything. If you know an empath or are one yourself, then you know exactly what I am talking about. The following are some of the challenges that these individuals have to deal with.

Their Feelings Can Be Flipped Easily

Imagine having the best day of your life. You are happy, energetic, and don't have a care in the world. You are on top of everything, and it seems that nothing can bring you down. Well, that is until something does. Of course, anyone of our moods can change quickly when something happens directly to us. This is not impossible. For an empath, though, nothing needs to happen to them directly. Once they are in the presence of someone who is emotionally distraught, their joyous mood can switch to a depressing mood instantly. Empaths are constantly shifting between various emotions due to the strong sensitivity they have with the environment. This puts them on a constant emotional rollercoaster. If they are in a group, the emotional fluctuations are even greater. From moment to moment, an empath will never know what his mood will be.

Emotional Fatigue Is Real

Dealing with our own emotions can be exhausting. Now, imagine adding several other people's emotions and having them be all over the spectrum. This can create heavy emotional fatigue.

Compassion Becomes A Burden

Empaths are often ridiculed for caring too much about other people. The truth is, it is hard for them to be any other way. They cannot turn off the compassion meter, which can become a burden after a while. Since an empath can feel suffering more than anyone else around them, it is difficult to not feel responsible for remedying it.

People Not Understanding Their Needs

Empaths are very likable, so people enjoy being around them. Many of them get invited out a lot. However, empaths need their alone time once in a while to recharge, but most people do not understand that. They believe they are just flaking on them, so they push them, even more, to go out. Unfortunately, most empaths will give in because they do not want to upset their friends.

Needing Time To Process Transitions

Empaths will have a hard time jumping from a high-stimulus to a low-stimulus environment. If they go from a crowded event to a small event, they will feel hollow for a while, trying to process the change. On the other hand, going into a suddenly crowded environment will overwhelm them.

It Can Be hard To Enjoy Yourself

Since you are always inundated with other people's feelings, it can be hard to enjoy yourself. You feel bad about feeling good, essentially, because you know that other people are suffering.

Get Taken Advantage Of

Because empaths care so much about other people, they often get taken advantage of. Certain types of people love to pounce on empaths because they know they can get away with a lot. We will talk more about these people later on.

Saying "No" Is Difficult

Empaths often feel guilty for saying "no," even though they need to say it more than anyone else. You are always willing to sacrifice your time and well-being for others until you hit a wall.

The struggles that empaths deal with are real. Unfortunately, their most unique qualities that are beneficial to other people have the most negative impact on them. Empaths must learn to use their characteristics in a way that helps others but does not overwhelm them. Otherwise, they will always live a life of suffrage.

What Creates An Empath

There is a wide range of reasons why a person becomes an empath. Some people are born with this mindset, while others develop it over time. This is the whole nature vs. nurture argument. Dr. Judy Orloff has described four different factors that contribute to empathy and becoming an empath.

- Some infants come out of the womb and are more sensitive to certain stimuli. For example, they cry more often and are extra sensitive to things like sound. Basically, people are born with different temperaments, which suggests that being an empath is a birthright to a degree.

- It is possible that there is a genetic component to being an empath. Many parents who are empaths often give birth to kids who are empaths too. However, this is not always the case, which means our genes are not the sole cause and may not have any connection in some cases.

- Children who are neglected or abused as a child often have their defenses torn down. They have experienced what it's like to be around a lack of sensitivity. In turn, they become extra sensitive as adults.
- Overly supportive parents can also create extra sensitive children. Children who take in many empath traits from their parents will carry them into adulthood.

Many researchers have found a significant amount of scientific backing related to being an empath. There is a specialized group of cells in our brains that are responsible for compassion. They enable everyone to mirror the emotions of the people close to them. These are known as mirror neurons, and they are thought to be hyper-responsive in empaths.

Empaths are also thought to have a stronger emotional contagion. This is a phenomenon where people can pick up on the emotions around them and then start feeling the same way. This can be seen in a room full of infants when one of them begins crying, and it sets off a cascade among the other babies too. Eventually, the whole room of infants is crying.

Finally, empaths are shown to have a higher sensitivity to dopamine, which is a neurotransmitter associated with the pleasure response. Dopamine is generally released when stimulated in some way. When an individual experiences a joyous moment, dopamine is released, which makes them even happier. Due to the higher sensitivity, empaths need less dopamine to increase their mood. This may explain why empaths are content being alone. They do not need a lot of external stimulation to feel good.

In summary, if you are an empath, then it is not something you can avoid. You are essentially stuck being an empath for the rest of your life. As you will see later on, this is not a bad thing. It is imperative, though, to manage the negative aspects of this quality, Which we will also get into more in the next couple of chapters.

Empaths And Toxic Relationships

While most people like empaths, the relationships they are in are not usually reciprocal. Meaning the compassion, kindness, and love that empaths give are not returned to them in the same manner. Of course, an empath would not expect these emotions to be displayed, but it's imperative to point out the lopsided relationships that many of them are involved in.

While many people take advantage of an empaths generosity, certain personality types take it to the extreme. These are the worst individuals for an empath to be around. They are collectively known as energy vampires and come in various forms. If you are an empath, you must recognize these energy suckers do that you can avoid them completely.

Energy vampires are the opposite of empaths. They lack any type of empathy, compassion, or emotional maturity, and do their best to take what they can from people. It is usually not through force, but with various manipulation tactics. Empaths, who are always willing to give, are the perfect victim for them. The following are different types of energy vampires that must be avoided.

The Victim

These vampires are always the martyr. They believe the world is out to get them and take no responsibility for their lives. They continually blame, manipulate, or blackmail to get what they want. The victim vampires feel unworthy in their lives, so they will work to garner sympathy by making you feel guilty.

The Narcissist

The Narcissist has no ability to show empathy and has no genuine interest in other people. They always expect to be put first, no matter the circumstances. They have giant egos that need to be fed, and they will always make sure not to go hungry. Narcissist vampires are dangerous because they will be very likable and charming at first to gain your trust, but then stab you in the back when it benefits them.

The Dominator

The dominator will make themselves feel superior through intimidation, whether physical or emotional. They are often loudmouths with rigid beliefs about how the world should be. Therefore, many of their viewpoints are archaic and can be seen as racist, sexist, or homophobic.

The Judgmental One

Judgmental vampire suffers from low self-worth. As a result, they project these feelings onto other people through shame and ridicule. Basically, they make themselves feel better by making you feel small.

The Innocent One

Unlike the other vampires, the innocent types are usually not malicious. They genuinely need help in their lives and are just looking for a hand. Their intent is not to harm anyone; they are just not emotionally strong enough to help themselves. That being said, you will still drain yourself if you are their constant rock to lean on. The key is to help but also to encourage self-sufficiency.

Unfortunately, many energy vampires are those who are closest to us, like family and lifelong friends. This makes it even easier to fall into their traps and get out energy sucked out by them. This makes it more imperative to be on high alert for their manipulative tactics.

The objective of this chapter was to paint a picture of what an empath is. Hopefully, you can visualize one in your mind. If you are an empath too, then you probably recognize many of the characteristics described here. Also, you have probably experienced the same setbacks. The remaining chapters in this book will focus on the positive aspects of being an empath and how you, as an empath, can share your gifts with the world, while also protecting yourself from harm.

Chapter 5: The Empath Blessing

In the previous chapter, I described in detail what an empath is and what challenges exist from being one. I admit that I probably did not paint the most appealing picture, but my goal was to make you aware of the specific empath traits so that you can recognize them within yourself and others. Once you do, then you can work on improving yourself by overcoming the obstacles that are in the way of your success.

The truth is, being an empath is a blessing because you bring so much value to the world. Some have described their abilities as paranormal, or as having a superpower. People rely on you because of the gifts you possess to be able to help them. The focus of this chapter will be to illustrate the positive impact that an empath can bring to those around them, in every facet of their lives. If you fall into this camp, just know that you are a very good addition to anyone's life.

Empaths As Leaders

Because of the unique personality traits an empath has, they are actually great leaders. They have a strong capability to create positive change within an organization. This is considering they don't allow themselves to be manipulated. The following are some of the top reasons that empaths can become successful leaders in any environment.

- They want to improve the world. Empaths are contributors, rather than takers, and want to improve human relationships by offering tremendous support.

- Empaths burden themselves with other people's issues, which may not be great in the long run, but can get a lot accomplished in real-time. Bearing this extra burden will often push empaths towards their goals.

- They have good relationship skills and can communicate better with those around them because of their deep understanding of the world.

- Their followers do not see them as intimidating, which means they are more willing to work with them.

- Empaths have a deep love for humanity, in general, so they do not discriminate against anybody.

- They look towards the future, not in the sense of making profits, but finding solutions that plague so many people.

- Even the most closed off and difficult people to work with will engage with an empath because they will provide a comfortable atmosphere to do so.

- They do not let success get to their heads, and they will not try to steal all the credit.

While empaths are not known for having strong personalities, they have endearing qualities that make them very likable and trustworthy. People are drawn to empaths, and this allows them to create successful teams with many different types of people. If empaths held more leadership roles, whether, in politics or business, the world might be a friendlier place.

Why Empaths Are Great Friends

Just like highly sensitive people, empaths have appealing personalities that make them great friends. As an empath yourself, just know that anyone is lucky to have you in their lives. Why do empaths make great friends? I will explain why.

Empaths Will Know When You're Not Well

Empaths will know stuff about you without you having to tell them. This is not in a creepy or intrusive way. They simply have the skills to pick up on various clues that you are unknowingly putting out. These abilities go beyond being intuitive and actually border on the paranormal. It is as if they can read your mind. As a result, an empath will know when you are upset, ill, tired, or going through any other negative emotion. There is no hiding your feelings when you are with an empath. Because they recognize the pain you are going through; they will have the compassion and understanding to help you get through it. If you have a problem, you can always count on your empath friend.

They Know The Right Things To Say

Because empaths are so good at picking up on the emotions of others, you rarely have to explain to them what you are going through. The chances are, they already know. This will save you a lot of pain and frustration, trying to explain what is wrong. Of course, if you want to explain it, an empath will listen with open ears.

When we are feeling negative, for whatever reason, it can be hard to get the point across to people because they are not going through our experiences. They are not living in our bodies. An empath will be by your side and will not ask unusual questions or completely miss the point about what you're saying. Finally, they will understand when to push forward with an issue and when to back off. In most cases, an empath will know what to say and the right time to say it.

They Can Protect You From Other People

There is something ironic to discuss here. Since empaths have such high compassion and kindness inside of them, they are willing to help almost anybody. On the other hand, an empath can help protect you from other toxic people. Because of their ability to understand people quickly, they can determine if a person is genuine or might have some ulterior motives. Therefore, if an empath has some unpleasant vibes about someone, it is in your best interest to listen.

Some people suggest not to be around anyone that an empath does not approve of. I will not go that far. However, never dismiss the feelings of an empath and always keep them in the back of your mind. Even if an individual seems perfect in every way, there might be some red flags you miss that an empath will recognize immediately. They will know if someone is dishonest and what their true intentions are. On that note, do not try to be dishonest with an empath because they will pick up on it quickly.

They Are Fun To Be Around

Being friends with an empath is an exciting experience because they are free spirits. They tend not to live in the norm and are always up for an adventure. If you're looking for a travel buddy, consider an empath because they are up for almost anything. You will have a blast. A word of caution: You may have to share your empath friend with other people because their personalities are attractive, even to strangers.

They Are Great Listeners

When you are speaking with an empath, you can be sure they are listening. They are not just listening so they can respond, but because they genuinely want to hear what you are saying. They will also help you come up with the best solutions since they understand you so well. However, if you are just talking to vent and are not looking for someone to solve your problems, an empath will understand that too and just listen without interrupting.

I want you to assess your current situation right now regarding your inner circle. Who are the types of people that you enjoy hanging out with the most? I want you to be completely honest with yourself. What personality traits do they carry? Do some of your best friends behave as empaths, at least partially? The chances are, those whom you genuinely enjoy being around possessed many of the innate attributes that are associated with empaths.

Seek out empath relationships, and you will not be disappointed. If you are an empath, then share your gifts with the world. Just make sure to keep yourself safe. I will discuss how to do this more in the next chapter.

The Empath As A Spouse

For the final showcasing of why being an empath is a blessing, I will discuss why empaths make great spouses. If you can find an empath as a partner, then you will be in a luckier place.

They Care About Making You Happy

With empaths, you do not have to worry about selfishness in a relationship. They want a happy life, and they understand that making their spouse happy is part of it. They are more concerned with having a genuine connection with their partners than they are with material possession.

They Make Amazing Parents

If you want children someday, then having an empath as a partner is a blessing because they make amazing parents. An issue that children deal with is that the adults in their lives don't understand them or pay attention to them. They often feel neglected and tossed aside. This will not be the case with an empath. They will be in tune with their children, just as much as they are with anyone else.

They Are Willing To Change For The Better

As a relationship grows, so must the people who are involved. Some individuals are so hardheaded that they are never willing to change. Empaths are so profoundly connected to the world and the people around them that they will recognize their shortcomings and will always be willing to work on them. If there are issues within a relationship, the empath will look inside of themselves and determine where they need to improve.

They Are More Tolerant And Understanding

Empaths understand that people are not perfect. They can also recognize the pain someone is experiencing on the inside. As a result, they are more patient, tolerant, and understanding of people's mistakes and shortcomings.

They Want You To Be Yourself

You do not have to put on a fake persona for an empath. They want you to be yourself. In fact, if you are trying to be fake, they will pick up on it quickly.

The Love Is Passionate

Empaths know how to make you happy. When they do make you happy, they will feel the same way. This will bring them a lot of joy and passion. The happier you are, the happier they will be. So, they will love you with great passion, and make you feel more accepted than anyone else can.

They Are Great At Working Through Disagreements

Since an empath can put themselves in your shoes, it is easier for them to see where you are coming from. They will be able to respond accordingly and work through disagreements more smoothly.

They Hold You Accountable

This may be one of the most important traits of being an empath. Since empaths really understand what you are going through, they will have compassion, but also know that you have the ability to fix it. As a result, they will hold you accountable for improving yourself and getting past whatever is harming you.

As you can see, an empath is a great leader, friend, partner, and pretty much anything else. As long as they are able to harness their power for the well-being of others while keeping themselves safe, they can do a lot of great things in this world. Don't be a stranger to an empath.

Chapter 6: Protecting Yourself

A knight in shining armor has the power to protect those who need him. However, without his armor, he will be harmed easily. The same holds true for an empath. An empath is a true blessing to the world, as we detailed in the previous chapter. However, without properly protecting themselves, an empath is at great risk for many negative consequences. Their mental and physical health, relationships, careers, and even personal safety can be affected, so they must take the proper precautions for their own well-being.

The focus of this final chapter will be about how an empath can protect themselves. I will go over some valuable tips and strategies to keep you safe so that you can continue to bless the world with your gifts. The reality is, once you burn out, you can no longer help others. This means that self-care is not just for you but also for the benefit of other people. The better you are to yourself, the better you can be to other people.

Protect Yourself Against Energy Vampires

While empaths can recognize a negative person because they are aware of people's true motivations, they still fall victim to toxic individuals. Their caring personalities can get the best of them, so they fall prey to people who use them the most. The obvious example here is energy vampires. These are any type of individuals who literally suck out your energy and make you feel drained. I described energy vampires in an earlier chapter, and now I will go over how to protect yourself as an empath from these energy stealers.

Realize They Exist

The first step in solving a problem is recognizing there is one. Energy vampires are a big problem for you if you are an empath. Empaths have a tendency to believe that all people are good and ignore the fact they are in a toxic relationship. Recall some of the characteristics I described for energy vampires and start realizing that bed people who want to take advantage of you do exist.

Keep A Journal Of Your Gut Instincts

Since empaths are highly intuitive, probably more so than anyone else, their gut instincts will tell them a lot about a person. As an empath, you must learn to listen to your gut instincts and never dismiss them, no matter how ridiculous they may seem at first. Also, after spending a lot of time with energy vampires, you can start losing the ability to believe how you feel. One thing these energy stealers are good at is manipulation.

When you are with someone, pay attention to what they are engaging in and write down how they make you feel inside. Pay special attention to how they treat a variety of people they encounter, like waitresses, flight attendants, and cashiers, etc. How an individual treats people who are not considered high on the status bar says a lot about who they are.

Have A Reality-Check Friend

A friend like this is an objective observer who has not been taken in by the energy vampire. They should be trustworthy and be able to their honest opinion about a person when your own judgment might be clouded.

Pat Yourself On The Back

Empaths often due not give themselves the credit they deserve, even though they are responsible for many of the good things around them. Instead, they deflect the credit onto someone else, effectively minimizing their own contributions. I don't want you to get a big head here, but I hope you can pat yourself on the back often recognize what you have accomplished. Write these accomplishments down on a piece of paper daily, so you have something visual to look at.

Put Yourself First

This should be the case no matter who you encounter in your life, but energy vampires are exceptionally good at making empaths feel guilty. They will use every manipulative tactic in existence to make sure they are at the forefront of your mind. They do not care about you unless you are doing something for them. So, make them stop caring. Whenever you feel like your in the presence of an energy vampire, take a step back. Leave the room completely if you have to. From here, remind yourself about your needs and that you deserve to live a joyful life. This will help keep you from falling into the vampire's trap.

Add "No" To Your Vocabulary

I don't care if you have to stand in front of the mirror all day repeating this word, but get as comfortable as you can saying the word "no." It is okay, and even necessary, to use this word once in a while. Empaths have a difficult time saying "no," and their knee-jerk reaction to anything is often "yes" without even considering their own feeling. I don't want you to automatically say "yes" to everything because you will not have the ability to set boundaries. If you have a hard time saying "no," at first, start with a lighter phrase like, let me think about it. Eventually, you can work yourself up as you feel comfortable. The main goal is t not be agreeable all the time.

Prioritize Your Own Quality Time

Set aside sometime every day for your own needs. Even if it is just 20 minutes, this time should be spent focused on your well-being and self-care. Do whatever makes you feel good at this moment, like meditation, reading, taking a bath, or going for a walk. Avoid things that might bring you stress, like social media drama, or watching the news. Stick to your guns about this self-care time, and do not let anyone interrupt it. Visualize all of your negative energy, disappearing into thin air.

Set Boundaries

Learn to set boundaries with people, or they will take up all of your time. As an empath, people will be vying for your attention because they know you will give it to them. You need to put the breaks on this mindset ASAP. I am not saying you can't help people. However, you need to put strict limits on how much time you will spend doing so, because you still need to fit in your self-care. If your friend needs help, set aside time when you can help them, but also place a strict time limit on the encounter. You cannot just be available any time of day for as long as they need it. This may sound insensitive, but it's really not. Your well-being is important too.

One of the ways to ensure you live a happy life as an empath is to keep toxic people away from you as much as they can. Vampires, like the many I have described, can sniff out the blood of an empath and dominate them into submission. If you are not careful, you will be under their control for the rest of your life. There may be times you cannot avoid toxic people; therefore, the techniques above can be used to distance yourself and avoid their tactics as much as you can.

Take regular stock of your friends too. The people in your inner circle should fill you up and make you feel good. If they are not doing that, then it's time to distance yourself or get rid of people completely. An energy vampire can infiltrate themselves into your life unsuspectedly. You must stay on high alert at all times for these individuals.

Harnessing Your Empath Power

Empaths have strengths that cannot be denied. The world needs these blessings now more than ever. This is why it's important to take care of your inner empath. We cannot afford to lose you. Once empaths learn how to harness their superpowers, they can become empath warriors and begin saving the world. Empaths who know how to save their energy are unstoppable because they know themselves well enough to practice self-care and stop absorbing the negative energy around them.

Going back to Dr. Judy Orloff, as an empath herself and someone who has researched the topic endlessly, she has come up with several strategies to harness your empath power and make you a true warrior in this respect. I encourage you to practice these techniques on a regular basis, so they become a habit for you.

- Express gratitude every day for what you have in life. Being grateful allows your mind to stay focused on positive energy by keeping you in the moment, rather than wasting energy worrying about the future.

- Practice different meditation techniques. There are many techniques out there that can help center you and make you in charge of your emotions. Mediation can take a while to master, but the initial goal is to reach a state of mindfulness

- Practice mindful breathing by focusing on your inhalation and exhalation. Breath in clarity and strength and breath out stress and negativity. Make sure you can feel your breaths down to your diaphragm. Practice these several times a day.

- Strengthen your intuition by learning to listen to it. Notice when your energy levels either increase or decrease when your around somebody. Stick with the people who make your energy levels go up.

- Practice loving yourself every day. Make sure to always engage in positive self-talk. How you speak to yourself plays a big role in your self-worth.

These exercises are simple and can start being used right away. When they become a regular part of your routine, you will be able to share your empath gifts, without being taken advantage of.

Best Careers For An Empath

To give yourself the best chance of winning, it is imperative to set up an environment that benefits you. You will never stop being an empath, and nor should that be your goal. However, it should be your goal to use your strengths in the best way possible. If you are like most people, then you need to work to make a living. It will behoove you to be in a setting that enhances your strengths and minimizes your weaknesses. The following are some of the best career options for empaths.

Nursing

Nursing would be a great career path for a naturally caring and compassionate person, like an empath. They will be using the skills they possess every day, providing the best care for people. Just be mindful that high-stress and fast-paced settings like the emergency room or the ICU can create some complications for the empath's psyche. However, this can be overcome with some practice and experience.

Artistic Careers

These include things like writing, painting, ceramics, or photography. Empaths are known to be creative individuals, so anything in this line of work will be great for them.

Psychologist Or Counselors

People in these careers need to be intuitive, kind, compassionate, and caring. They need to have a deep desire to help people and often have to read between the lines to get the real answers. An empath possesses all of these qualities, so they would excel in this career path.

Veterinarian

Empaths are not just great with people, but also animals. In fact, there is a subset of empaths who can relate to animals on a very deep level, almost as if they can read their thoughts and communicate with them. This is great since animals cannot speak for themselves. An empath who becomes a vet can help heal and comfort sick animals, and also soothe their worried owners.

Musician

Just like with an artist, an empath can let out their emotions and creativity in this line of work. There will also be opportunities to play so many different instruments, as well.

Teacher

There are very few people who need empathy in their lives more than children. Children cannot always express their needs with clarity, so having someone who understands them well is a huge plus. They will gravitate towards an empath because they feel comfortable around them. With proper motivation and support, a teacher could change a student's entire life.

As an empath, if you are looking for a career where you will thrive and none of the above interests you, that's okay. There are plenty of opportunities out there that will require your skillset. While you can succeed anywhere, jobs that require compassion, care, patience, intuitiveness, and kindness, while also being less fast-paced, might be the best pathways to take.

Being Kind To An Empath

I want to end this book by speaking to those on the opposite side. If you have gotten through this book and realized that you are not an empath, that's okay. The chances are that you know an empath, or will meet one at some point. I want to help you understand some important issues about being an empath so that you can bring the best out of them, and they can bring the best out of you. As I mentioned before, an empath will be one of the best people in your life, if you understand how the dynamics of the relationship will work. Here are a few important facts to remember.

- Empaths cannot change who they are. They can work on ways to protect themselves, so they are not used and abused, but they cannot stop being extra kind, compassionate, and caring.

- Empaths cannot be caged and become shut-ins. They have to get out and explore; otherwise, they will lose their zest for life.

- Empaths need time alone, so make sure they get it.

- They see life much differently than others, so give them support.

- They know if you're lying, so always be honest, even if it hurts.

- They love to laugh, so make them laugh often.

- They will be on an emotional rollercoaster, and so will you.

In summary, do not be with an empath if you can't handle life being different every day. If you can, then get ready for the time of your life.

PART III

Chapter 1: Self-Care Is the Best Care

"It is so important to take time for yourself and find clarity. The most important relationship is the one you have with yourself."

-Diane Von Furstenberg

Self-care is any activity that we deliberately do to improve our own well-being, whether it is physical, emotional, mental, or spiritual. The importance of taking care of one's self cannot be denied, as even health care training focuses on making sure healthcare workers are caring for themselves. If you do not take care of yourself, eventually, every other aspect o your life will fall apart, including your ability to help others.

This is a very simple concept, yet it is highly overlooked in the grand scheme of things. People lack the tendency to look after themselves and put their needs before anyone else. Good self-care is essential to improving our mood and reducing our anxiety levels. It will do wonders for reducing exhaustion and burnout, which is very common in our fast-paced world. It will also lead to positive improvements in our relationships.

One thing to note is that self-care does not mean forcing ourselves to do something we don't like, no matter how enjoyable it is to other people. For example, if your friends are forcing you to go to a party you rather not attend, then giving in is not taking care of yourself. If you would rather stay in and watch a movie, then that's what you should do, and it will be better for your well-being.

How Does Self-Care Work

It is difficult to pinpoint exactly what self-care is, as it is personal for everybody. Some people love to pamper themselves by going to the spa, while others enjoy physical activities like hiking, biking, or swimming. Some individuals take up art or other hobbies, like writing or playing a musical instrument. These activities are all different but will have the same type of benefits for the individuals engaging in them.

The main factor to consider when engaging in self-care is to determine if you enjoy the activity in question. If not, then it's time to move on. Self-care is an active choice that you actually have to plan out. It is time you set aside for yourself to make sure all of your needs are met. If you use a planner of any sort, make sure to dedicate some space for your particular self-care activities. Also, let people who need to know about your plans so you can become more committed. Pay special attention to how you feel afterward. The objective of any self-care activity is to make yourself feel better. If this is not happening, then it's time to change the activity.

While self-care, as a whole, is individualized, there is a basic checklist to consider.

- Create a list of things you absolutely don't want to do during the self-care process. For instance, not checking emails, not answering the phone, avoiding activities you don't enjoy, or not going to specific gatherings, like a house party.

- Eat nutritious and healthy meals most of the time, while indulging once in a while.

- Get the proper amount of sleep according to your needs.

- Avoid too many negative things, like news or social media.

- Exercise regularly.

- Spend appropriate time with your loved ones. These are the people you genuinely enjoy and not forced relationships.

- Look for opportunities to enjoy yourself and laugh.

- Do at least one relaxing activity a day, like taking a bath, going for a walk, or cooking a meal.

Self-care is extremely important and should not be an anomaly in your life.

How Does Self-Care Improve Self-Esteem and Self-Confidence?

To bring everything full circle, self-care plays a major role in improving self-esteem and self-confidence. It is easy to see how taking care of yourself will also make you feel better about yourself overall. All of these are actually inter-related, and a lack of one showcases a lack of the other. While caring for yourself also improves your self-esteem and self-confidence, not having self-esteem or self-confidence also leads to a lack of self-care. Basically, you believe that you are not good enough to be taken care of.

People with high self-esteem and self-confidence value themselves as much as they value others, and have no issues with making sure they're taken care of. They realize that it does not make them selfish or inconsiderate to think in this manner. Even if other people try to make them feel that way, a self-confident person will just brush off the criticism. An important thing to note is that when you take care of yourself, it does not mean you don't care about other people. It simply means you have enough self-love to not place yourself on the backburner.

Many people work so hard to try and please everyone else. This is one of the telltale signs of low self-esteem. While they're busy worried about other peoples' needs, their own get neglected, which will wear them down over time. The more they're unable to please someone, the harder they will try. What people in this situation don't realize is that some people are impossible to please, and it is not their responsibility to please them. That is up to the individual.

Poor self-care will eventually lead to poor self-image. It is possible that a person already has this initially. Self-care includes taking care of your hygienic and grooming needs. If you don't take the time to make yourself look good, this will significantly impact the value you place on yourself. When you are t work, among your friends, or just walking around town, not feeling like you look good will ultimately make you feel like you don't belong anywhere. Your confidence levels will plummet due to this.

Your health is another aspect to consider. Poor self-care means bad sleeping habits, unhealthy diets, lack of exercise, and more self-destructive behaviors. Your poor health practices can result in chronic illnesses down the line, like heart disease or diabetes. Once again, diminished health will lead to reduced self-confidence and self-esteem. Ask yourself now if putting other people ahead of you is worth it? I've got some news for you. The people who demand the most from you are probably looking out for themselves first.

The less a person takes care of themselves, the more their self-esteem and self-confidence will decline. It turns into a vicious downward cycle. This is why it is important to focus on all of these areas equally. When you find yourself neglecting your own self-care practices, it is time to shift your direction and bring your attention back to your needs. Ignoring your needs will ultimately lead to your fall. We will discuss specific practices and techniques for improving self-care in the next chapter.

Chapter 2: What Does Good Self-Care Look Like?

Good Self-Care Practices

The following are some ways that good self-care will look like. If you find yourself having these qualities, then you are on the right path.

Taking Responsibility for Your Happiness

When you engage in self-care, it is truly self-care. This means you only rely on yourself, and nobody else, to make sure your needs are met. You realize that your happiness is no one else's responsibility but your own. You alone have the ability to control your outcomes. As a result of this independence, you will develop the skills and attitude you need to care for your own physical, mental, emotional, and spiritual well-being.

You Become Assertive With Others

People often take assertiveness for rudeness. This is not true, but if people believe that standing firm for what you want is rude, then that's their problem. Once you reach a certain mindset where self-care is important to you, then you will be unapologetically assertive. This means you have the ability to say "no" with confidence and stand by it. "No" is a complete sentence, and people will realize that quickly when they hear it from you.

You Treat Yourself As You Would a Close Friend

It's interesting how we believe that other people deserve better treatment from us than we do ourselves. We have a tendency to put our best friends in front of us, no matter how detrimental it is to our lives. This behavior stops once we engage in proper self-care. At this point, you will treat yourself as good as, or even better, than you treat your most beloved friends.

You Are Not Afraid to Ask for What You Want

Once you learn to take care of yourself, you also see your value increase within your mind. This means having an understanding that your voice, opinion, and needs matter, just like anybody with high self-esteem and self-confidence, would. As a result, you will not be afraid to ask for what you want, even if you might not get it.

Your Life Is Set Around Your Own Values

Once you practice self-care, you learn to check in with yourself before making important decisions. You always make sure the choices you are about to make line up with your purpose and values. If they go against them, then it's not a path you choose. This goes for the career you choose, where you decide to live, and the relationships you maintain in your life.

While all of the traits are focused on self, but it will lead to better relationships with other people too. When you practice self-care, you are in a better state in every aspect of your being. This gives you the ability to take care of and help those you need you, as well, Self-care is not an option, but a necessity, and it must never be ignored. Taking care of yourself is not selfish, no matter what anybody tells you. If someone tries to make you feel guilty over this matter, then consider distancing or removing them from your life. You are not obligated to maintain relationships with people.

Chapter 3: Demanding Your Own Self-Care

We went over the importance of self-care, and now we will focus on making it a reality in your life. If you want self-care to occur, you must be willing to demand it. The world is full of people who expect you to be at there beck-and-call every moment of the day. Some of these individuals are those who are closest to us, like friends or family members. This can make it harder to make our demands heard, but there is no way around it. Taking care of yourself is not an idea you can budge on. It is extremely important. We will go over several ways to maintain your ability for self-care in your life and provide detailed action steps to help you progress in this area.

Setting Healthy Boundaries

One of the biggest obstacles to self-care is other people who surround you. These are the true selfish individuals, whether they realize it or not, who believe they can barge in on your life and deserve all of your attention. They will take advantage of you, and if you are not careful, they will completely gain control of your emotions, and even your life. For proper self-care to occur, you must set firm and healthy boundaries with people. The following are steps that need to become mainstays in your life.

Identify and Name Your Limits

You must understand what your emotional, physical, mental, and spiritual limits are. If you do not know, then you will never be able to set real boundaries with people. Determine what behaviors you can tolerate and accept, and then consider what makes you feel uncomfortable. Identifying and separating these traits will help us determine our lines.

Stay Tuned Into Your Feelings

Two major emotions that are red flags that indicate a person is crossing a barrier are resentment or discomfort. Whenever you are having these feelings, it is important to determine why. Resentment generally comes from people taking advantage of us or feelings of being unappreciated. In this instance, we are likely pushing ourselves beyond our limits because we feel guilty. Guilt-trips is a weapon that many people use to get their way. It is important to recognize when someone is trying to make you feel guilty because they are way overstepping their boundaries. Resentment could also be due to someone imposing their own views or values onto us. When someone makes you feel uncomfortable, that is another indication of a boundary crossed. Stay in tune with both of these emotions.

Don't Be Afraid of Being Direct

With some people, setting boundaries is easy because they have a similar communication style. They can simply read your cues and back off when needed. For other individuals, a more direct approach is needed. Some people just don't get the hint that they've crossed a line. You must communicate to them in a firm way that they have crossed your limits, and you need some space. A respectful person will honor your wishes without hesitation. If they don't, then that's on them. Your personal space is more important than their feelings.

Give Yourself Permission to Set Boundaries

The potential downfalls to personal limits are fear, self-doubt, and guilt. We may fear the other person's response when we set strong boundaries. Also, we may feel guilty if they become emotional about it. We may even have self-doubt on whether we can maintain these limits in the long run. Many individuals have the mindset that in order to be a good daughter, son, parent, or friend, etc., we have to say "yes" all the time. They often wonder if they deserve to have boundaries and limits with those closest to them. The answer is, yes, you do. You need to give yourself permission to set limits with people because they are essential to maintaining healthy relationships too. Boundaries are also a sign of self-respect. Never feel bad for respecting yourself.

Consider Your Past and Present

Determine what roles you have played throughout your life in the various relationships you have had. Were you the one who was always the caretaker? If so, then your natural tendency may be to put others before yourself. Also, think about your relationships now. Are you the one always taking care of things, or is it a reciprocal relationship? For example, are you always the one making plans, buying gifts, having dinner parties, and being responsible for all of the important aspects of the relationships? If this is the case, then tuning into your needs is especially important here. If you are okay with the dynamics of the relationship, then that's fine. I can't tell you how to feel. However, if you feel anger and resentment over this, then it's time to let your feeling be known, unapologetically.

Be Assertive

Once again, this does not mean being rude, even though some people will interpret it that way. Being assertive simply means being firm, which is important when reminding someone about your boundaries. Creating boundaries alone is not enough. You also have to stand by them and let people know immediately if they've crossed them. Let the person know in a respectful but strong tone that you are uncomfortable with where they're going, and they need to give you some space. Assertive communication is a necessity.

Start Small

Setting boundaries is a skill that takes a while to develop, especially if it's something you've never done before. Therefore, start with a small boundary, like no phone calls after a certain time at night. Make sure to follow through; otherwise, the boundary is worthless. From here, make larger boundaries based on your comfort level.

Eliminating Toxicity and Not Caring About Losing Friends

If you plan on making self-care a priority in your life, I think that's great, and so should you. However, some people will have a problem with this. People don't always like it when their friends, family members, or acquaintances, etc., put themselves at the forefront of their lives. Once again, that is their problem, not yours. What is your problem, though, is distancing or even eliminating these individuals from your life. We will go over that in this section because part of self-care is eliminating toxicity from your life and not feeling bad about it.

Don't Expect People to Change

While everyone deserves a chance to redeem themselves, there comes the point where we must accept that people cannot change by force. They have to find it within themselves to make this change, and it is not our responsibility to do so. You may yearn to be the one who changes them, but it's usually a hopeless project. Toxic individuals are motivated by their problems. They use them to get the attention they need. Stop being the one to give it to them.

Establish and Maintain Boundaries

I already went in-depth on this, so I won't revisit it too much here. Just know that toxic people will push you to work harder and harder for them, while you completely ignore your own needs. This is exhausting and unacceptable. Create the boundaries you need with these individuals based on your own limits.

Don't Keep Falling for Crisis Situations

Toxic people will make you feel like they need you always because they are constantly in a crisis situation of some sort. It is a neverending cycle. When a person is in a perpetual crisis, it is of their own doing. They often create drama purposely to get extra attention. You may feel guilty for ignoring them, but remember that their being manipulative and not totally genuine.

I am not saying that you can't ever help someone who is going through a hard time. Of course, you can. Just don't start believing that you're responsible for their success or failure.

Focus on the Solution

Toxic individuals will give you a lot to be angry and sad about. If you focus on this, then you will just become miserable. You must focus on the solution, which, in this case, is removing drama and toxicity from your life. Recognize the fact that you will have less emotional stress once you remove this person from your life. If you let them, they will suck away all of your energy.

Accept Your Own Difficulties and Weaknesses

A toxic person will know how to exploit your weaknesses and use them against you. For example, if you are easy to guilt-trip, they will have you feel guilty every time you pull away from them. If you get to know yourself better and recognize these weaknesses, then you can better manage them and protect yourself. This goes along with creating self-awareness, which we discussed in chapter two. When you accept your weaknesses, you can work on fixing them and balance them with your strengths.

They Won't Go Easily

Recognize that a toxic individual may resist being removed from your life. Actually, if they don't resist, I will be pleasantly surprised. They may throw tantrums, but this is because they can't control or manipulate you anymore. They will even increase their previous tactics with more intensity. It is a trap, and you must not fall for it. Stay firm in your desire to leave and keep pushing forward. If they suck you back in, good luck trying to get out again.

Choose Your Battles Carefully

Fighting with a toxic person is exhausting and usually not worth it. You do not need to engage in every battle with them. They are just trying to instigate you.

Surround Yourself With Healthy relationships

Once you have removed a toxic person, or persons, from your life, then avoid falling into the trap with someone else. Fill your circle with happy and healthy relationships, so there is no room for any toxicity. Always remember the signs of a toxic person, so you can avoid them wholeheartedly in the future.

How to Focus on Self-Care

Now that we have worked to set boundaries and eliminate toxic people from our lives, it is time to focus on ourselves and the self-care we provide. The following are some self-care tips, according to psychologist, Dr. Tchiki Davis, Ph.D.

Pay Attention to Your Sleep

Sleep is an essential part of taking care of yourself. You must make it part of your routine because it will play a huge role in your emotional and physical well-being. There are many things that can wreak havoc on your sleep patterns, like stress, poor diet, watching television, or looking at your phone as you're trying to fall asleep. Think about your night routine. Are you eating right before bed or taking in a lot of sugar and caffeine? Are you working nonstop right up until bedtime? Have you given yourself some time to wind down before going to sleep? All of these factors are important to consider, as they will affect your sleep patterns. If you can, put away any phones, tablets, and turn off the television at least 30 minutes before you plan on going to bed.

Take Care of Your Gut

We often neglect our digestive tract, but it plays a major role in our health and overall well-being. When our gut is not working well, it makes us feel sluggish, bloated, and nonproductive. Pay attention to the food you eat as it will determine the health of your gut. It is best to avoid food with excess salt, sugar, cholesterol, or unhealthy fats. Stick to foods that are high in fiber, protein, healthy fats, and complex carbs. Some good options are whole grains, nuts, lean meats, fruits and vegetables, beans, and fish.

Exercise and Physical Activity Is Essential

Regular exercise is great for both physical and mental health. The physical benefits are obvious. However, many people do not realize that exercise will help the body release certain hormones like endorphins and serotonin. These are often called feel-good hormones because they play a major role in affecting our mood in a positive way. The release of these hormones will give us energy too, which will make us want to exercise more. Once exercise becomes a habit, it will be hard to break. Decide for yourself what your exercise routine will be, whether it's going to the gym, walking around the neighborhood, or playing a game of tennis.

Consider a Mediterranean Diet

While this is not a dietary book, the Mediterranean diet is considered the healthiest diet in the world because of its extreme health benefits. The food groups and ingredients that are used will increase energy, brain function, and has amazing benefits like heart and digestive tract health. The food also does not lack flavor, which shatters the myth that healthy food does not taste good.

Take a Self-Care Trip

Even if you are not much of a traveler, getting away once in a while can do wonders for your mental health. So often, our environment will make us feel stressed out, and it's good to remove ourselves from it for a couple of days. You do not have to take a trip abroad here. Of course, that is certainly an option. A simple weekend trip is perfectly fine. Just get yourself out of your normal routine and be by yourself for a while.

Get Outside

Nature and sunlight can be great medicines. It can help you reduce stress or worry, and has many great health benefits. Doing some physical activity outside, like hiking or gardening, are also great options.

Bring a Pet Into Your Life

Pets can bring you a lot of joy, and the responsibility they come with can boost your self-confidence by having to care for another living creature. Dogs are especially great at helping to reduce stress and anxiety. Animal therapy has been used to help people suffering from disorders lie PTSD, as well.

Get Yourself Organized

Organizing your life and doing some decluttering can do wonders for your mental and emotional health. Decide what area of your life needs to be organized. Do you need to clear your desk, clean out the fridge, or declutter your closet? Do you need to get a calendar or planner and schedule your life better? Whatever you can do to get yourself more organized, do it. Being organized allows you to know how to take better care of yourself.

Cook Yourself Meals At Home

People often neglect the benefits of a good home-cooked meal. They opt, instead, for fast-food or microwave dinners. These types of meals will make you full but will lack in essential nutrients that your body needs. Cooking nutritious meals at home will allow you to use the correct ingredients, so you can feel full and satisfied. Cooking alone can also be great therapy for people.

Read Regularly

Self-help books are a great read. However, do not limit yourself to these. You can also read books on subjects that you find fascinating or books that simply provide entertainment.

Schedule Your Self-Care Time

Just like you would write down an appointment time in your planner, also block out specific times for self-care activities. Stick to this schedule religiously, unless a true emergency comes up. This means that if a friend calls you to go out, you should respectfully decline their request and focus on yourself.

Chapter 4: How to Be Happy Being Alone

The final section of this book will focus on being alone and how to be happy about it. When you start engaging in self-care, you will also be spending much more time by yourself. A lot of people have a hard time dealing with this concept, especially if they're used to being around people all the time. However, for proper self-care, you have to be okay with being alone once in a while.

Accept Some Alone Time

The following are some tips to help you become happy with being alone. Soon, you will realize that your own company is the best kind.

Do Not Compare Yourself to Others

We are referring to your social life here. Do not compare to others, and do not feel like you must live as others do. If you do this, you may become jealous of a person's social circle or lifestyle. It is better to focus on yourself and what makes you happy. If you plan on spending significant time alone, then you cannot pay attention to what other people are doing.

Step Away From Social Media

If strolling through your social media page makes you feel left out, then take a step back and put it away for a while. During self-care moments, you are the focus, not what is happening with others online. Also, what people post on their pages is not always true. Many individuals have been known to exaggerate, or even flat-out lie on social media platforms. You may be feeling jealous or left out for no reason. Try banning yourself from social media for 24-48 hours, and see how it makes you feel.

Take a Break From Your Phone
Avoid making or receiving calls. Let the important people in your life know that you will be away from your phone for a while, so they don't worry. When you are alone, really try to be alone.

Allow Time for Your Mind to Wander
If you feel unusual about doing nothing, it is probably because you have not allowed yourself to be in this position for a while. Carve out a small amount of time where you stay away from TV, music, the internet, and even books. Use this time to just sit quietly with your thoughts. Find a comfortable spot to sit or lie down, then just let your mind wander and see where it takes you. This may seem strange the first time, but with practice, you will get used to the new freedom.

Take Yourself on a Date
You don't need to be with someone else to enjoy a night out on the town. Take a self-date and enjoy your own company for a while. Go to a movie by yourself, stop by a nice restaurant, or just go do an activity you enjoy. If you are not used to hanging out alone, give it some time and you will become more comfortable with it. Take yourself on that solo date.

Exercise
We have mentioned exercise and physical activity a lot, but that's because it has so many great benefits related to self-care. Exercising will uplift your mood, and make it more enjoyable to be by yourself. Those feel-good hormones will provide a lot of benefits during these times.

Take Advantage of the Perks of Being Alone

Some people have spent so much time with other people that they've forgotten the perks of being alone. There are many to consider. First of all, you do not have to ask anyone's permission to do anything; you will have more personal space, can enjoy the activities you want to do, and don't have to worry about upsetting anyone. If you want, you can even have a solo dance party in your living room, Tom Cruise style. There are many advantages to being alone, so use them.

Find a Creative Outlet

It is beneficial to use some of your alone time to work on something creative. This can be painting, sculpting, music, writing, or any other creative endeavors. In fact, you can get out the watercolors and start fingerpainting. Creativity will bring a lot of joy into your life. It will make you happier about being alone.

Take Time to Self-Reflect

Being alone will give you the opportunity to self-reflect on your life. You won't care so much about being alone when you are coming up with important answers to your life.

Make Plans for Your Future

Planning out your life for five or ten years down the line will give you something important to do, and something to look forward to. Alone time is the perfect opportunity to determine these plans.

Make Plans for Solo Outings

Plan your solo outings based on what you like to do, whether it's a farmer's market, hiking, riding your bike, or going camping alone. Mak plans that will excite you, and you will be taking care of yourself while also being okay alone.

There are numerous topics that we went over in this chapter, but they all relate back to one theme: Self-care. Always remember that to take proper care of yourself, you must consider the following ideas:

- Setting Boundaries
- Avoiding and ridding yourself of toxic people
- Focus on yourself and your needs
- Be okay with being alone

Focus on these areas, and you will be demanding your own self-care without ever apologizing for it.

PART IV

Chapter 1: Energy Healing- The Key to Holistic Health

Understanding the impacts of energy imbalances and corresponding physical, mental, spiritual health

How many times have you, or another adult in your life, said the words "I just don't have the energy I used to have."? Most adults know the feeling of looking at the energy children have as they run about, enjoying life, exploring their surroundings, and never seeming to grow tired. Many of us are left reflecting back on the distant past when we, too, had such energy and wondering where it went.

From the time children enter school, they begin to be presented with expectations. Stand in a straight line, raise your hand, don't talk while the teacher is talking. Each year, the level of responsibility and expectation seems to increase. While rules, regulations, and individual responsibility are important for a functioning society, there are numerous expectations and social pressures put on people as they grow, which can be incredibly harmful.

It is generally around middle school when children become more acutely aware of their bodies and societal beauty standards, which tell them what they "should" look like. Children are likely to become aware of the trends, such as which clothes the "cool kids" are wearing. The endless battle to feel like enough begins, and can lead to a plethora of issues with self-esteem, eating disorders, and mental illness. In addition to the basic societal pressures to be accepted and considered attractive, many children are also faced with difficult situations at home where their own needs are not being met, they are having to provide for and protect themselves in the only ways they know how, avoid abusive parents, care for younger siblings, or worry about if they'll have anything to eat that day. Even if children have a relatively healthy home life, this is the age when they will begin to become aware of the issues that plague their family (every family has issues) whether this is divorce, an alcoholic parent, the death of a pet or loved one, etc.

We live in a society that thrives off of consumerism. We are flooded with images of how the next vacation, new pair of shoes, nicer car, nicer house, or perfect partner will make us happy, and all of the things we need to change about ourselves in order to fulfill those things. Eventually, all the energy we had as a child starts going towards maintaining our image in society, trying to have all the "best" life has to offer (which always happens to be everything we do not have), and attempting to be as "successful" as possible in the eyes of society and other people. With no time to rest in the present moment, recharge, and appreciate what we already have, it is no wonder, so many of us are completely drained of energy. In such a fast-paced society that discourages breaks, our energy will become depleted, and we will find ourselves thrown out of balance and unable to obtain true happiness and well-being. Over time, this depletion and imbalance can lead to a sense of spiritual disconnection, extreme mental health issues, and an increased risk of physical pain, illness, and even earlier death.

Chapter 2: Energy Healing and Overcoming Suffering

Energy and Grief/Trauma

Every human being knows that loss is a natural part of life. The one certain thing in life is that we, and everyone we know, is going to die. However, in such a fast-paced society, we are often given a very short grace period before being expected to swallow our grief and "move on" when we lose those closest to us. It is not abnormal for people to receive a bereavement period of only a few days before being expected to be back in the classroom or office and be fully functional. There is very little space for the grief journey, and most people are expected to harbor their feelings and keep their grief to themselves.

The grief process is expansive and incredibly energy draining. When we don't receive the adequate support from those around us, or adequate space to heal, our body begins to break down piece by piece. The empty spaces within us will swallow us up into states of depression, numbness, isolation, and pure exhaustion. Just like a wound being denied the correct treatment and care, the wounds of unresolved grief will fester and leave us feeling completely drained of energy and vitality for life.

Unresolved trauma also has an incredibly destructive impact on the body. Trauma can occur as a result of grief itself, as well as emotional or domestic abuse, accident or illness, war, sexual assault, childhood maltreatment, etc. The body holds trauma in various places, and the brain switches over from the logical ability to discern safety and danger into an easily triggered emotional state. An overactive emotional brain loses the ability to think clearly, make decisions, and recognize threats. People who have unresolved trauma are likely to be easily triggered and deal with unexplained outbursts of anger, fear, relationship issues, reckless behavior, and health problems. When trauma sits in the body unresolved, the brain is unable to understand that the traumatic event has ended. Therefore, it will stay in a consistent fight-or-flight state, which is incredibly draining and will leave the body with no energy. Not only will trauma victims experience low energy levels, but they will also experience severe issues maintaining positive relationships and overall well-being.

Energy and Mental Health

There are numerous factors that can contribute to mental health issues. As previously discussed, societal issues and unresolved grief and trauma can yield higher levels of anxiety, depression, and PTSD. It is also very common for people to suffer from mood disorders, personality disorders, disordered eating, substance abuse, etc. The list is long for psychological ailments and how they happen, and it has been proven that 1 in 3 people will be diagnosed with a mental illness in their lifetime. Even without a specific disorder, most people will have periods of life where their mental health suffers greatly.

No matter what a person's struggle with mental health looks like, or what they are doing (or not doing) in terms of treatment, the body expends a lot of energy when a part of it is unwell.

Daily Energy Regulation

No matter what it is in your life that is causing you to feel depleted, it is vital to pay attention to the energy fields within the body and identify the areas of greatest pain and imbalance. In the spectrum of health, people often take measures such as going to see the doctor, therapist, or grief counselor, taking medication, and making lifestyle changes such as finding a hobby or increasing exercise. However, a piece that is commonly overlooked in the healing journey is healing energetically. No matter how much you invest in your mental, physical, emotional, and spiritual health, if your energies remain imbalanced, it is impossible to reach a state of full wellness. That being said, energy healing is the missing piece in most people's quests for holistic health.

In many cases, it can be beneficial to seek the help of energy healers, massage therapists, and reiki, craniosacral therapy, or bodywork practitioners. These practitioners are trained in getting in touch with your energy centers and helping bring them back into balance through healing touch, body movements, and visualization techniques. If you are dealing with energy imbalance, seeing a practitioner can be an excellent investment in unlocking your highest levels of health and joy in life.

It is also possible to use a variation of the body scan mediation from chapter 3 to check in with your energy levels on your own. By taking notice of the sensations in each area of your body, you can come closer in touch with any area of your body where you experience regular pain, tension, or other unpleasant feelings. This is often a sign of imbalance or trapped energy. Additionally, the tense and release technique in each area of the body can yield healing and balance by releasing negative energy and tension. It is important to check in with yourself daily, asking your body where energy may be trapped or depleted and what you can do to replenish yourself.

Chapter 3: The Daily Energy Healing Journey

Understanding Your Energy Field: Daily Energy Healing Meditation with Journaling (Week 5)

There is a great variety when it comes to human energy fields. People experience varying levels of sensitivity to the energy of other people and the environment. Some people are incredibly in tune with "vibes"; others are empaths who feel the emotional experiences of others on a deep level, while still others experience very little of either. There is also a lot of variation in the way people recharge energetically, as well as what depletes them. In the common case of introverts and extroverts, for example, introverts need time alone to replenish their energy and feel balanced, while extroverts recharge in stimulating environments with other people around. One of the first steps to protecting your personal energetic field is to understand how it works.

Understanding Your Energy Field Journal Prompt (Week 5):

When you feel exhausted and not like yourself, which activities are most likely to replenish your energy? Do you enjoy a night out with friends? Yoga? A walk in the park? Leisure reading? Finding a new adventure? Taking a bubble bath? Listening to your favorite music on blast? List 5-10 activities that help you gain balance and feel energized.

Now, make a list of the things that make you feel most drained. These can be large things, like a specific task at your job, or small things like doing the dishes. You may find that you feel drained if you spend too much time alone or, consequently, when you spend too much time around other people.

When it comes to activities that make you feel drained, ask yourself to what extent that specific thing is necessary in your life. If you find yourself feeling drained from spending too much time around other people, for example, you can easily make a change by scheduling more "nothing time" or "alone time" into your days and taking the time you need to replenish. Household tasks and daily responsibilities are necessary, but by being aware of the ones that drain you the most, you can bring more attention to the process and doing what you need to replenish energy before or after.

Protecting Your Energy Field: Daily Energy Healing Meditation with Journaling (Week 6)

Close your eyes and ask yourself, "what does my energy field look like?" Write down any specific colors, textures, shapes, or patterns of movement.

Once you have an image in your mind of your energy field, ask yourself, "What does it look like for outside energies to enter my field?" Write down what healthy and unhealthy outside energies look like.

Then ask yourself, "How can I regulate the energies entering my field? What does it look like when I decide what I will let in?" Describe this process.

Finally, ask yourself, "How does my body feel when I regulate what I allow to enter my energy field?" Write down everything that comes to mind.

Healing Through Trapped Emotion Release: Daily Energy Healing Meditation with Journaling (Week 7)

In our society, we are often faced with life circumstances that force us to repress our basic human emotions. It is very possible for anger, rage, or grief to become stuck in the body because it is considered "impractical" to have those reactions in public. Similarly, we often hear about people being described as "annoyingly happy" or "overly emotional." Most of us are taught not only to manage our emotions but to distance ourselves from them and react emotionally only in certain contexts. Additionally, we tend to suppress negative emotions such as fear, shame, inadequacy, and insecurity, for the purpose of appearing like we have everything together. Between life events and societal expectations, it is very easy for the emotions we suppress to become trapped in our bodies, which can create adverse health effects, negatively impact our relationships, and keep us from living our best lives.

Begin by making a list of as many emotions as you can think of

Run down the list of emotions one by one, asking yourself, "Is there anywhere in my body I am holding *particular emotion*?"

Write down the emotions you feel are trapped. Take some time to journal about how certain emotions arose, or times when you felt you had to suppress your emotions.

With each emotion you have labeled as being trapped, write: "I give myself permission to release this *particular emotion*

Cultivating Self-Trust in your Healing Journey: Daily Energy Healing Meditation With Journaling (Week 8)

No matter what you do in your life, there will always be people who don't understand the choices you make, or who judge the path you are on. When it comes to renewing and protecting your energy, there is no room for anyone else's opinions or emotions in regards to your journey. It requires a great deal of self-trust to go your own way and let what other people think about it roll off your back. For this reason, it is vital to begin everyday establishing a sense of self-trust with your own journey and energy management skills. The following four journal questions will help you direct your energy before going about your day.

What are you most grateful for today?

What are your intentions for how you will direct your energy today?

What are your fears/things you perceive as a potential threat?

What are your commitments to yourself and the world?

Mini Meditation Toolbox: 25 Quick and Easy Energy Restoration and Protection Meditations

One-Minute Energy Cleanse

- This meditation is useful if you find yourself with a person or in a specific situation that feels negative or energetically draining. You do not need to be alone to complete this meditation

- Pause where you are and allow yourself to take a few deep, cleansing breaths

- Focus exclusively on your breathing; you may close your eyes or leave them open

- Feel the inner power within the core of your body, around your abdomen. Remind yourself that you are in control and have the power to maintain balance.

- As you inhale, pull love, light, and peace into your body

- As you exhale, breathe out pain, annoyance, and toxicity

Energy from the Earth

- Begin by entering a space in nature. This can be on the beach, in the mountains, near a river, in a garden, by the lake, or in your own yard

- If possible, slip your shoes off, so your bare feet are in contact with the earth

- Start with a few cleansing breaths, taking note of everything you see, hear, smell, and feel in your environment
- Placing the soles of your feet on the ground, begin to breathe, pulling the energy from the earth up through your body
- Remember that you are One with the nature that courses around you. Allow it to heal what is broken within you and leave you feeling rejuvenated

Re-Centering Head Hold (3-5 minute meditation)

- Close your eyes and place the palm of one hand horizontally across the crown of your head, and the other palm across your forehead (over the energetic points of the Crown and Third Eye chakras). This position can be done while standing, sitting, or lying down.
- While clutching your head in this position, bring attention to any sensations in your body. What needs your attention most right now?
- Allow yourself to come back to the present moment, feeling grounded in your body and in your experience
- Breathe in awareness, focus, and comfort, exhaling anxiety and distraction
- When you open your eyes, notice how you feel grounded in your space

The Cloak of Protection

- This meditation is useful for energy protection before going out into the world, whether that is to work, the supermarket, an appointment, etc.

- Although you do not know what kinds of energies you may encounter, or which people may try to take your energy from you, remind yourself that you are in control of your own energy and that you have the capacity to protect yourself

- Close your eyes and imagine a dark-blue, almost black cloak made of a soft, thick material like a velvet night sky. The cloak is full-length with a hood to protect all of your chakras.

- Imagine a ray of light outlining the cloak in whatever color(s) feel most magical, protective, and authentic to who you are

- Set off into the world knowing that you are safe within yourself and your energy cloak and that you do not need to be afraid

De-Cluttering your Space

- When energy is lacking or out of balance, the spaces we live in are likely to reflect that imbalance with clutter and messiness. The more we feel like we "don't have our lives together," the more likely we are to have a messy desk, dishes piling up in the sink, laundry that still needs to be folded, or a car that has not been cleared of trash

- Such spaces do not allow for peace and mental clarity and can be even more draining to come back to after a long day

- Dedicate yourself to one area of your life to de-clutter. This can be your kitchen, your car, your bedroom, etc. Close your eyes before beginning and take a few deep, cleansing breaths to approach the task calmly

- Begin to address all of the clutter in the space, not only picking it up but putting it into a designated area where it can be organized and easy to find

- You may find that you want to create a special shelf or move some furniture around to make the space less cluttered. As you go, notice the energy that continues to unfold in your body

- When you finish, place a "clutter basket" in your room, the car, the living room, etc. where you can compile all the clutter throughout the day and put it away before bed

De-Cluttering your Mind (5-minute meditation)

- Close your eyes and begin to breathe deeply

- Ask yourself, "What is taking up the most space in my mind right now?"

- Bring your attention to whatever it is that is distracting you, and why it makes you feel out of control

- Breathe into that situation, saying, "I have control over this situation, and I am not going to let it spill out into the rest of my day. I am clearing this space."

The Energy-Ownership Mantra

- This meditation is ideal to perform in the morning, or before going out to interact with the world or other people

- Sit in a place where you feel energized (on the porch, in your meditation corner, etc.)

- Close your eyes and begin to breathe, checking in with any unresolved emotions or senses within the body

- Now begin to picture your energy field. Say to yourself: "My energy field is my sacred space, and other energies will only permeate it when I allow them to."

- Breathe into this thought for several moments

- Now, bring this thought into your mental space: "I have the wisdom to discern what belongs to me and what belongs to other people. I can be empathetic and attentive to other people's emotions, struggles, and opinions without assuming responsibility for them."

Epsom Bath Energy Renewal

- Begin by selecting your favorite scented Epsom salts. You may also customize your bath with petals, oils, and candles as according to the healing plants, herbs, and oils listed in Chapter 4

- Run a hot bath, letting your Epsom salts and other elements saturate the water

- Customize your space with the light of candles, meditative music, and anything else that makes you feel at peace

- Find a comfortable position inside the tub. Close your eyes, and feel your entire body relax into the heat and gentle movement of the water.

- Begin to conduct a body scan, feeling entirely vulnerable to this moment at peace with only yourself

- Ask your body, "What do I need right now?"

- The water should be hot enough that you begin to sweat (be sure to have a glass of water nearby). As you sweat, imagine your body purging itself of every blockage, every impurity, and every negativity

Sealing your Energy Field

- Close your eyes and begin to breathe

- Bring the image of your energy field to your mind. You may picture a wall, a bubble, or a glowing ring of light (this image may also differ depending on the day)

- Picture what other energies look like, floating around your field like particles in an atom. Say to yourself, "I am in control of what comes in."

- Imagine yourself recognizing people who are trying to take your energy or bear their burdens. Imagine any fear, anger, or resentment you may feel.

- Say to yourself, "No, not today." Imagine your bubble becoming impermeable, your wall being sealed, your glowing ring of light rejecting anything that does not belong inside
- Allow yourself to feel empowered over your energy, without feeling any resentment or judgment towards those who once posed a threat

Building your Sanctuary

- Sit down and close your eyes, beginning to breathe into yourself
- With each breath, ask yourself, "What makes me feel safe?" Repeat three times.
- Switch the phrase to "What makes me feel at peace?" Repeat three times.
- Switch the phrase to "What makes me feel loving?" Repeat three times
- Switch to "What makes me feel joy?"
- Lastly, ask yourself, "What makes me feel renewed?"
- When you ask yourself these questions, you may see certain crystals, scenes in nature, types of music, plants, aromas, decorations, activities, or color schemes. Take note of whatever comes to mind.
- Use these things that come to you in meditation to mindfully cultivate a space for yourself to come into every day when you need time to recharge. This can be a meditation corner, a spot

in the backyard, or any other space that is sacred to you and provides feelings of security and rest.

Cultivating Non-Reaction

- This meditation can be used when encountering a stressful situation, having a difficult conversation, or otherwise entering a state of nervous or angry energy

- Before responding to whatever the negative stimulant is, breathe into the moment. Close your eyes if needed.

- Tell yourself, "I can choose not to expend energy on this interaction. I can choose to move peacefully into the next moment."

- Feel the tension within you melt away as you make the choice not to internalize the stress of the situation or the negative energy coming at you

Boundary Setting

- Find a quiet place to sit and self-reflect. Breathe into the moment

- After you have settled into your breath, ask yourself, "What people, circumstances, or tasks drain my energy and leave me feeling agitated or exhausted?"

- Allow the answers to rise into your consciousness at will. Meditate on every name, every task, every circumstance which makes you feel tense and throws your energy out of balance.

- With each name, circumstance, and task, say to yourself, "This *person, place, thing* has no power over me. I can maintain my energy in spite of it."

- Next, ask yourself, "Where do I need to draw the line with this *person, place, thing*?"

- Listen to your intuition tell you what your boundaries should be. Perhaps, this looks like gently cutting off a toxic person, or limiting your interaction time with them. It could be quitting a job that is no longer good for you or asking for accommodations to make your environment more positive. It could be telling someone who expects you to bear their burdens that their energies are no longer your responsibility. Or, perhaps it is to establish a self-care activity to do directly after a draining task.

Trigger Awareness

- If your energy has ever been thrown out of balance by trauma, there are likely still factors of your environment that can strike at any time, causing your body to react in the same way it did at the time of the trauma.

- Breathe into the moment, asking yourself, "what elements of my environment cause me to lose control of my logic and feel afraid, helpless, irrational, in pain, or otherwise unbalanced or unhealthy energetically."

- These elements are called "triggers." Bring your awareness to these triggers, simply allowing them to be there without judgment.
- Say to yourself, "that moment in time is over. I can now release myself."

Energetic Tapping

- Begin by determining 3-5 affirmations or manifestations for the day ahead ("I manifest peace," "I am content," "I am present," "I manifest energy," "I am growing," "I manifest healing," "I manifest loving-kindness," etc.)
- Breathe deeply, pondering the affirmations/manifestations
- Choose your first manifestation/affirmation. With your index and middle fingers on both hands, begin tapping lightly on the crown of your head, repeating the manifestation or affirmation three times
- Move to the temples, tapping and saying the manifestation/affirmation three times
- Repeat at the inner corners of the brow bone
- Repeat just above the brow line
- Repeat at the top of the cheekbones
- Repeat below the ear lobes at the crest of the jawbone
- Repeat at the top of the chest
- Repeat on the left wrist, then switch to the right wrist

- Switch to the next affirmation/manifestation and go through the process again, staying in touch with your breath throughout

Listening to your Intuition

- Find a space where you feel completely comfortable and relaxed
- Begin to breathe deeply, coming into the present moment
- Ask yourself, "What does my inner self need me to know right now?"
- Keep breathing, holding space for whatever answer arises
- If necessary, you can ask follow-up questions to yourself, like "Is there any threat I need to be prepared to protect myself from?" or "How can I best love the world today?" Or "What do I need to do to take care of myself today?"
- Continue to breathe and hold space, trusting that your heart will guide you to make the correct decisions for yourself

Memory Reclamation (specifically for healing of trauma victims)

- Find a space where you feel totally safe and undisturbed. It is best to do this meditation on a day where you can invest in self-care and rest.

- Begin to breathe, telling yourself, "I am safe. I am safe. I am safe."

- Allow the memory of a particularly traumatic event to come to your mind. Continue to breathe, telling yourself, "I am safe."

- Pay attention to the details of that memory. What do you see? What do you hear? What do you feel?

- As the memory progresses, allow it to release its energetic hold on your body. Tell yourself, "That was then. This is now. I am safe."

- Feel the trauma release its hold on you, restoring itself to a basic memory of the past

Defining your Needs

- Sit in a peaceful place, breathing into the moment

- Bring attention to any pain or unrest within your body. Without judgment, allow it to be there, asking if there is anything you should learn from it.

- Generally, where there is pain or unrest, there is a need being left unmet. Ask yourself, "What is it that I need?"

- Allow your needs to arise into your consciousness ("I need a day off for my mental health," "I need a trip into nature," "I need a bath," "I need a warm, nourishing meal," "I need to go to sleep early," etc.)

- Breathe into each need, envisioning yourself meeting that particular need

- Ask yourself, "Is there anyone else I need to make aware of these needs?"

- Envision yourself having a calm conversation about your needs with your boss, your partner, your family, or a friend. Envision them, reacting gently and yourself feeling better understood and supported.

- Continue to breathe into your capacity to meet your energetic needs and make those needs known to others.

"Nothing Time"

- Set aside a minimum of one hour of time with absolutely nothing scheduled

- Sit down, breathing into the moment. Tell yourself, "this is my time. I have nowhere to be, nothing to do; I do not need to feel rushed."

- Allow your deepest intuition to guide your next step. Do whatever comes to mind first

- While you proceed with your "nothing time," allow your breath to guide every move

Discovering your Support System

- Bring your attention to the present moment, focusing on your breath

- Ask yourself, "Who of the people I know understands and embraces me for who I truly am?"

- Breathe with each name that comes up, allowing loving-kindness and appreciation for that person to flow through your body

- Ask yourself, "Who in my life encourages me to reach my full potential?

- Repeat the action of breathing with each name that arises

- Ask yourself, "Who in my life do I feel most at rest with?"

- Repeat the action of breathing with each name that arises

- Continue to breathe, saying to yourself, "These are my people. This is my support system. I will allow myself to lean on them when I need to."

Glowing Love-Energy

- Find a restful position and begin to breathe

- Imagine the aura of your energy field. How big is it? What color is it?

- Say to yourself, "I am pure love. I have room to love the entire universe and everything in it."

- Continue to repeat this phrase with every breath. Picture the aura expanding and glowing brighter

Jaguar Spirit Animal Protection

- Bring yourself into the present moment with deep breathing
- From the depth of your being, say, "I call on the spirit of the jaguar to protect me."
- Feel the reverberations of the jaguar's protection through your body, aiding you in repelling negative energy and toxicity
- Imagine a fierce, beautiful guard of your energy field, encircling you with fierce love and security

Energetic Breathing (1-3-minute meditation)
- Take some space away from your everyday life (in the bathroom, in the car, etc.) to just breathe
- Implement the 5-5-7 breathing technique
- With every breath in, say to yourself, "I breathe in pure energy."
- With every breath out, say to yourself, "I breathe out *exhaustion, *toxicity, *negativity, etc."
- Continue until you feel the tingle of pure energy coursing through your veins

Energetic Dancing/Movement
- Find a space where you can be alone and feel completely secure
- Play a song that stirs your soul and emotions, causing you to have a visceral reaction in the body each time you hear it

- As the song begins, close your eyes and deep breathe, maybe swaying back and forth slightly

- When you feel ready, release your body to move as it feels led. No choreography, no expectations, simply letting the movement of the moment lead your body into a state of pure surrender and release

- Surrender entirely to the moment, trusting your body to release any tension or trauma

- Give your body the space and freedom to heal, coming into energetic harmony

The Art of Saying "No"

- Close your eyes and begin to breathe deeply

- Begin to consider the things that drain your energy. Perhaps you have a tendency to overcommit or find yourself stuck in a relationship or circumstance that no longer serves you. Breathe with each of these places where you feel stuck

- Say to yourself "I have the power to say 'no.'"

- Imagine yourself having the necessary conversation, turning down the opportunity, or simply choosing to remove yourself from the situation

- Feel the power of saying no and being in full control of where you place your energy

The Restorative Power of Letting Go

- Breathe deeply, cultivating a sense of full peace and security
- Ask yourself, "Where are the parts of me that I need to get back?"
- Take notice of every person or place that comes to mind as still having a part of your energy and your essence
- If there are any feelings of melancholy, nostalgia, resentment, shame, or anger, allow them to be there, breathing as they flow through you
- Say to yourself, "I release this *person or place*. I reclaim what they have that is rightfully mine."
- Continue to breathe into this empowerment

PART V

Chapter 1: Anxiety, The Monster Within

"I know what it's like to be afraid of your own mind."

- Dr. Reid from Criminal Minds

- Obsessing over small worries that constantly distract you
- Whirling from action to action to try to quiet your minds' nagging
- Attempting to drown out anxious thoughts in any way possible, solemnly wishing they would just disappear

If you are here with us today, you are likely living through all the above and more, trying strategy after strategy to eliminate these causes of stress. Or, perhaps you are seeking help for a loved one that has anxiety that is weighing them down. Or, maybe you are simply here to feed your curiosity of what anxiety is and how it plagues the mind. No matter, I work with anxiety every day and have spent the majority of my existence on Earth immersed in it.

My grandfather was such a worrier that he physically shook, *constantly*. His body would tremble from the overwhelming magnitude of worry that lurked within him. He was a burly southern man who favored anything outdoors and fishing. His long, curly locks framed his rounded face with an always generous smile. When he was at his warmest, he was a magnet to others. However, his most natural state was when he was in worry mode.

What did he worry about? Anything and everything. He was worried about all the typical things that grandparents do; along with I'm sure many countless unspoken things.

"Do you have enough to eat?"

"Do you need the salt or pepper?"

"Are you comfortable? Too hot? Too cold?"

Even though he was a burly man, his voice was soft, so anyone listening had to lean in. I think he like the intimacy it afforded. Whenever we were all at ease, he was at ease.

Us grandkids always ran with the joke, *"Grampy, can we pass you the salt and pepper?"* His anxiousness would disappear with a smile and flush of embarrassment. We did this to show our appreciation, to relieve the tension and let him know he was never a burden and that we loved our big burly gramps for who he was.

Our gramps was a people-person, always curious and invested in others. I have very clear memories of coming home and hearing his low but small voice in the answering machine, *"Hello, it is just me again. Just checking in to see how you are coming along…"*

He needed that regular assurance that everything was, in fact, alright and always preferred to hear it firsthand. And if he could do things for someone, that was even better.

As Gramps aged, his anxiety escalated and he became less able to use it in a constructive manner. There were less and fewer ways for him to release his anxious feelings, to the point he became crippled with worried on a daily basis. When I search into where my own anxiety stemmed from, a picture of Grampy always pops into my mind. When I studied anxiety in graduate school, his shaking body was a perfect analogy. The more time I spent exposed to the study of anxiety in the human body, I began to understand my grandfather better than he likely understood himself most days. I also realized how persuasive anxiety was throughout our family's history. It was what set the foundation for me to deeply understand how much anxiety affected emotions and behaviors.

Thankfully, no one else in my family shook as much as my grandfather did from anxiety; however, looking back, anxiety was the hub of all the spectrum of extremes my family endured. My mother was motivated by her anxiety, while my father was like a balloon, letting stress and anxious feelings build up until he popped with rage.

While no one in my immediate family was ever diagnosed with an anxiety disorder, I can still imagine that just like so many others, they would have felt the same shameful stigma that comes along with all mental health problems, thinking that something is wrong with them. They were simply noticing things in their lives and felt deeply about them; they just didn't have the tools and knowledge to cope with the overload of information.

Through my years as a psychologist, I have gained a different perspective on anxiety and how it alters thoughts and feelings. I have come to see anxiety as a resource and seek to embrace its value in our everyday lives.

Anxiety derives from the feeling of realizing that something we genuinely care about may be at risk, as well as the arrival of resources that we need in order to protect it. Anxiety prompts us to look closer and pay better attention to messages we receive and helps us to gain the motivation we need to take control of situations. The key to getting back a life driven by anxiety and fear is to take control. This is where I have used my knowledge to help others, in ultimately steering them in a different direction of gaining back their willpower.

How Anxiety Overshadows Everyday Lives

Living in denial, second-guessing your every move, thinking ill thoughts about your future, living in fear of the unknown; all these things can overshadow a person's life and lead to constant anxiety.

If you or a loved one is plagued by anxiety, you have probably endured panic attacks and constant negative nagging in your head on a regular basis or have a phobia of some kind feel ashamed of their "sickness."

Anxiety has the power to make everyday folks feel insane, even though they truly aren't. Just like with all people, some days are better than others, but those who experience symptoms caused by these mental ailments typically have a higher count of bad than good days.

They often feel that they are always under a dark cloud that pours rain, but that rain is not made up of just water. Those drops from the sky above their head are created from startling visions, disturbing logic, feelings of worthlessness and/or hopelessness and looks that they receive from both loved ones and strangers when they truly believe they are in a type of personal crisis or feel as if they are about to be pushed over the edge. This is just a small portion of what it is like to live with anxiety.

What is Anxiety?

Anxiety, in its simplest form, is a bodily reaction to unfamiliar or dangerous environments and scenarios. Everyone has the tendency to get anxious from time to time and feel distressed or uneasy. This happens perhaps before a big game, performing in front of an audience or right before a huge job interview. Feeling anxious is a natural response that our bodies can feel during moments like these. Anxiety gives us the boost we need to be consciously aware and alert to prepare us for certain situations.

Our body's "fight-or-flight" response is under this umbrella of reactions. But imagine feeling like this *all* the time, even during the calmest of moments?

Picture a life where you have issues concentrating on everyday tasks, where you may be frightened to leave the safety of your home when you cannot fall or stay asleep because your mind is in a constant whirlwind of thought? Living with an anxiety disorder is debilitating. That is putting it lightly in some cases.

Causes of Anxiety

Every one of us is unique, which means even common disorders, like anxiety and depression, resonate within each of us differently, as well as why we are living with anxiety, to begin with. There are several key factors that cause anxiety disorders to grow in the mind:

- Chemistry of the brain

- Environmental factors

- Genetics

- How we grew up

- Life events

The factors listed above are the basics that lay the groundwork to potentially be a victim of anxiety, but those below mixed with any of those above could set one up to be someone that is at a higher risk than others in the development of an anxiety disorder:

- Alcohol, prescription medication or drug abuse

- Chemical imbalances in the body and/or brain

- History of anxiety that runs in family bloodlines

- Occurrence of other mental health issues

- Physical, emotional or mental trauma

- Side effects one has on particular medications

- Stress that lasts an extended amount of time

The feelings and thoughts that anxiety promotes within a sufferer create a bubble that creates lonely thoughts and feelings, which is why it is no surprise that anxiety disorders are the most common of mental illnesses with the U.S, with **over 40 million American adults** living with one of these disorders as we speak.

If it is any consolation, you are by no means alone when it comes to feeling the way you do. There is still a lot of research being put into finding out why anxiety plagues so many individuals, its specific causes and why it resonates within individuals in such vast ways.

Signs & Symptoms of Anxiety Disorders

All of us will experience anxiety in our lives; it is a normal response to stressful life events. But as you have learned so far or experienced for yourself, these symptoms can become much larger than the events of stress them and can interfere heavily with a happy, healthy way of life.

Below are the most common symptoms of anxiety:

- **Worrying** that is disproportionate to the events that trigger it and is intrusive, making it challenging to concentrate on everyday tasks.

- **Agitation** that causes fast heartrates, sweaty hands, dry mouth, etc.

- **Restlessness** or feeling on edge with a constant uncomfortable urge to move that won't go away.

- Becoming **easily fatigued**, either in general or after a panic attack.

- **Difficulty focusing** on everyday tasks.

- **Issues retaining short-term memory** which results in a lack of performance in multiple areas of life.

- Becoming **easily irritable** in the day to day life.

- Constantly having **tense muscles** that may even heighten anxious feelings.

- **Issues falling and staying asleep** due to continued disturbances in the sleep cycle.

- **Panic attacks** that produce overwhelming sensations of fear.

- **Avoidance of social situations** due to a fear of being judged, humiliated, or embarrassed.

- **Extreme fears** about very specific situations or objects that are severe enough to interfere with normal functioning.

Understanding Social Anxiety

Imagine at random times, feeling so uncomfortable in particular situations to the point of not being able to process what is happening around you or difficulty breathing. Welcome to the life of those that deal with social anxiety. Social anxiety is classified by a major discomfort with social interactions as well as a fear of judgment. There are more than 15 million Americans that deal with this in their everyday lives that struggle with the awkwardness of social settings.

Symptoms of Social Anxiety

The main symptoms of this form of anxiety are feeling intensely anxious when in social situations or avoiding them altogether. Many sufferers have a constant feeling that 'something just isn't right', but are never able to pinpoint it.

As you can imagine, these people have a twisted way of thinking that includes false beliefs of situations and negative opinions from others. Many people fear the interaction days or weeks before the event, which means that social anxiety can manifest in other physical symptoms, such as:

- Sweating
- Shaking
- Diarrhea
- Upset stomach
- Muscle tension
- Blushing
- Confusion
- Pounding of heart
- Panic attacks

The key aspect of social anxiety to remember is that even though these folks have a fear of speaking or interacting with others, it doesn't mean they have nothing to say.

Below are things that those who suffer from social anxiety would say to others to help them understand how they feel:

"I do not want this and I cannot help it. It is not just a bit of nervousness that comes and goes. It is constant stress and living in a world that you start to not recognize."

"In my ability to speak right, I lack confidence. There are many times I want to say something, but hold back because I am afraid of how dumb it may sound or that I will be misunderstood. I am afraid of speaking in groups, phone calls, and approaching people the most.

"I am terrified of people's reactions when I do scrounge up the courage to finally speak."

"My anxiety socially is not a constant. There are certain situations that cause me more anxiety than others. It is a fluid disease."

"Many times, people don't realize that those with this anxiety disorder are suffering because of the lack of physical symptoms. Just because you cannot tell there is something wrong, doesn't mean there isn't."

"I cannot help how ridiculous it may seem."

"It hurts to know that people take my anxiety personally instead of just helping me out."

"I wish I had a social life, but my anxiety won't let me; I am not anti-social."

"It may look like I am zoning out from time to time, but I am actually practicing positive self-talk and breathing techniques to stay calm and ward off a panic attack."

"I am not trying to be standoffish, rude, or snobby, even though it may seem that way when I refuse hugs or don't wish to speak. I simply get overwhelmed and overstimulated easily. All I ask for is respect."

"I want people to break the ice and speak to me first. I am genuinely a nice person, I just have a fear I am unable to control."

"I wish more people understood that when I say I cannot come, it is because the situation I was invited to feels 'impossible', not because I don't feel like it."

"When I leave early, I am not being disrespectful. I just need to fight off a meltdown with some alone time."

"Social anxiety is not 'shyness'; that is like comparing a stab wound to a paper cut." No one experiences social anxiety in the same way. Each day is like living a life of constant fear; worrying about the disapproval of others, rejection, not fitting in, etc. They are bound to be anxious to enter or begin a conversation.

Chapter 2: Acknowledging Your Anxiety

While the numbers of those that suffer from anxiety in the United States alone exceed 40 million, you may feel alone in your symptoms as well as what triggers them. Things that set off those anxious thoughts and feelings are a bit different for everyone who experiences anxiety. It is important to take time to focus on yourself and learn what things provide you with peace or create tension in your life.

Common Anxiety Triggers

- The hustle and bustle of everyday life. Life is always busy and there never seems to be time to slow down.
- The inevitable fact that we are only growing older.
- Driving, especially on freeways with many cars or across bridges.
- Not living up to the expectations that we set for ourselves.
- The sense of uncertainty. When we are not on control of situations we tend to freak out a bit. This comes from a lack of communication and anxiety making conclusions for us.
- Ambulance, fire or police sirens.
- Stresses at work – Not performing well enough, not having enough time during the course of the workday to get things done, etc.
- Simply thinking about what triggers your anxiety can be a cause for anxiousness in itself.
- Being too hot is often times directly associated with being claustrophobic.
- The inevitable part of life known as death. This especially goes for individuals who have experienced much loss in their lives.
- Being alone.

- The possibility of finding out that people do not like you as much as you think they do.
- Being judged or verbally attacked.
- Large crowds.
- The inability to predict the future. Those with anxiety often dislike surprises.
- Trying new things.
- Being far away from home or other places familiar to you.
- When many people speak to or at you all at once.
- The struggles that your children may face at school.
- Money! This is a big one. Whether it is saving for a big event such as a wedding or purchasing a home or car, the process of paying monthly bills while still trying to save money for other things.

Getting to the Root Causes of Your Anxiety

What many of us do not realize is that many causes that trigger our anxieties to flare up are actually self-produced. While you can blame your situation, family, friends, etc. for you distress, you are the one who perceives life as it goes on around you. The way you view it, analyze and take it all is all dependent on you. The root reasons behind the curtains of 'Play Anxiety' are usually caused by one of the following reasons.

Negative Self-Talk

It is said by research conducted by behavioral specialists that upwards of 77% of all the things we think to ourselves is quite counterproductive and negative. What we don't realize is that we are being our own worst critic and a detriment to ourselves. Learn to become consciously aware of the way you speak to yourself.

Write down any sort of negative thoughts for a day and then each day forward practice transforming those negative words or thoughts into a happy, loving one towards yourself. While it may feel weird at first, it will become second nature to you once you practice it for a while. Your self-talk is just as important of a daily habit as any other.

Unrealistic Expectations

Sometimes we simply just have too high of expectations that create a high world that we struggle to reach. Expecting those to be perfect and remember all the details about you is just ridiculous. If your expectations fly way above you, you are more than likely missing out on grand opportunities and are unable to truly recognize the good things that are happening that you should be celebrating.

This goes for the expectations you have for yourself as well. Are they actually realistic? If not, how can you go about making them more reasonable and achievable?

The "Should" Thoughts

Do you find your brain thinking that you "should do this" and you "should do that" often? Have you ever just taken a moment to actually find the reasoning behind why you "should"? Telling yourself that you should is equivalent to telling yourself that you are not good enough. It leads to negative self-talk fast and should be avoided. Make a positive list of the things you should do or become. Are they yours or someone else's expectations?

Taking Things Too Personally

Those with anxiety feel like many things that occur are actually their fault when in reality they more than likely had nothing to do with someone's disgruntled behavior or a glare they received. Learn to not take things too personally because you never know what may be happening in the life of other people. "We are all in the same game, just different levels. Dealing with the same hell, just at different devils." If you think you are the cause of someone's actions, speak up and ask instead of just assuming. This will get rid of a lot of assumptions that go into negatively feeding your anxiety.

Our minds are wired to believe the things that we tell it the most. If we are always engaging in negative self-talk, expect too much of others or ourselves, do things we just merely think we "should" do or worry about those around you, your brain will act negatively as well. It is all about building a positive foundation for your frame of mind for all those thoughts of yours to dwell in. In order to unlock the door to happiness and less stress and/or anxiety, it is time to get thinking in a happy manner!

Pinpointing Your Anxiety

While you can take all the time in the world to read information in regards to relieving anxiety via the internet, books or other media, unless you take action and decide that you truly want to make a change to lower your anxiousness, it will never happen. I am an anxiety sufferer and back just a couple years ago it engulfed my everyday life and drowned me more than a few times.

I finally over time came up with a process that assisted me greatly with determining what triggered my anxious thoughts so that I could get a grip on my life and yield them from continuously taking over my personal life.

- **Stop** – When those feeling of anxiousness begin to hit you, stop and take a moment to make a mental note of what you are doing right at that moment. This is easier said than done, for you might be in the middle of a task, conversation, etc. But it is beneficial to take just a moment to identify when you began to feel anxious.

- **Identify** – Recognizing the onset of anxiety will help you come to the

134

conclusion of what actually causes it for you personally. If you develop the capability to notice triggers and feelings when they start to dwell, you can put a stop to them faster. Many people don't realize they are feeling anxious until their symptoms are outrageously taking over them. Over time, you will be able to catch on more quickly what is threatening your happiness and overall well-being.

- **Write** – As you become an expert of taking moments to make mental notes of why you feel anxious, I find that at the end of the day I write down the events during my day, both the goods one and those that triggered my anxiety. I keep a notepad on my cellular device so that I am quickly able to access it to jot down notes at the moment and then write them down on paper before heading to bed. Be sure to write down as many details as possible – what you are thinking, experiencing and feeling, etc.

- **Analyze** – At the end of the week is when I choose to review what I have written in my anxiety notebook. You can review it at the end of each day, week or month, but I do not recommend waiting any longer than that. I wait at least a couple days to a week so that I can see the pattern that my thoughts made. When you are aware of these patterns you are better able to focus on the causes of anxiety and avoid them.

- **Possibilities** – There are numerous things that you can make the scapegoat when it comes to feeling anxious. If you have adequate knowledge of these ideas, you can review patterns and conquer anxiety. Anxiety in many cases is situational. If you are anxious being in unfamiliar surroundings, expose yourself to these types of circumstances a little time. If your causes are more based on the way you think and view the world, learn to engage in positive self-talk. Once you have a pattern written out, you will be less anxious just by the fact that you have some idea and control over your anxiety situation overall.

Chapter 3: Trauma and Anxiety

The journey of life is exciting, scary, ridiculous, confusing and worth it all at once. But there are times that we all go through some type of emotional distress, whether it be mere sadness, rapid anxiety, addictions to outside influences, obsessions with things or people, compulsions we have a hard time controlling, behaviors that are self-sabotaging, physical injuries, anger, and bleak moods, among the hundreds of other things we go through, think and/or feel.

It is important to learn ways to cope when it comes to hard times, no matter the time frame. Something psychologically downgrading can happen in a matter of mere moments and leave you scarred for the rest of your life. Some people seek out help from other individuals who are professionals at understanding the human mind, but others wish to find help within them. Having the knowledge to help yourself is not an easy feat. It may be easy to read pages upon pages of books and self-help websites that provide information, but it is much harder to put those words into actions.

The world is a much different place now than it was just a decade or two ago. Technology has advanced so rapidly that some of us are overwhelmed with it all, especially the consequences that we receive, whether from our own actions or that of another being who acted upon a current mood. Human beings are not the robots that we seem to want to create so badly these days. We are emotionally driven individuals with a lack of having the knack to help ourselves in times of need and/or trouble.

The worst thing about the constant rise of this distress is the fact that there is no one age group or certain targeted individuals that are more likely to go through it. It is happening clear from late grade school levels all the ways into senior living years. Students have much more stress with perpetual levels of testing and pressure to be better. Employees live their hard-earned careers always fighting to make their way up the ladder with not much reward. Older individuals are continuously having their wages and retirement that they worked their entire lives for whisked away.

It is a dog eat dog world out there with a lot of room to make mistakes that can cause even more friction in our personal lives. With the constant pressure to be better than the next, our society has taught us maybe how to be more proficient in terms of getting things done at school or work, but many of us have forgotten the person that is truly important: OURSELVES. If we do not take care of our emotional health, detrimental things can occur. Below are some signs that you may be experiencing emotional distress. Some of the symptoms may surprise you.

Childhood Trauma and Sensitivity to Anxiety

Trauma during childhood can impact our entire lives. According to the Journal of Affective Disorders, children who experience traumatic situations are much more likely to have anxiety and depressions and fall victim to alcohol and drug abuse. The same study found that females are more susceptible than males to develop anxiety, even with the same rates of trauma.

If left untreated, trauma during childhood can have effects that last throughout someone's entire life. They are likely to developmental disorders that branch out to much more than just anxiety as well.

Common Anxiety Disorders Caused by Trauma

Common anxiety disorders that are caused by traumatic events are:

- Panic disorder
- Obsessive Compulsive Disorder (OCD)
- Post-Traumatic Stress Disorder (PTSD)
- Body Dysmorphic Disorder

- Agoraphobia
- Social Phobia(s)

As you can imagine, trauma anytime throughout your life can play a major part in the development of anxiety and other mental disorders in your lifetime.

Chapter 4: Grabbing your life back from anxiety

Now that you have acknowledged that life could be better and have learned how to interpret why you live a life filled with anxiety, it is time to take your life back, pronto! There is a variety of methods we will discuss in this chapter that can help you gain back the confidence you need to live life to the fullest.

Managing Your Emotions

Emotions are a natural human phenomenon. , and are very present in pressing and painful times. Every day we are driven by some force of emotions:

- We take chances because we get excited about new opportunities
- We cry because we are hurting and make sacrifices for those we love

Those are just a couple examples of emotions; they dictate our actions, intentions, and thoughts with authority to our rational minds. Emotions can become a real problem, however, when we act too fast or we act on wrong types of emotions, which cause us to make rash decisions.

Negative emotions, such as bitterness, envy, or rage, are the ones that tend to spiral out of control the most, especially when triggered. It only takes one slip of our emotions to totally screw up the relationships in our lives.

If you have issues controlling your emotions, here are some steps that you can implement into your everyday life that will help you regain rationality, no matter what challenging situation you are facing:

Don't react right away

You are more likely to make mistakes when you react right away to emotional triggers. When reacting right away to these triggers, you are likely to say and do things that you will later regret.

Before acting on emotions, take a deep breath to stabilize your impulses.

Breathe deeply for just a couple minutes and you will be able to feel your heart rate return to normal. One you become calmer, remind yourself that feeling this way is just temporary.

Find healthy outlets

Once you have managed your emotions, you need to learn how to release that build up in the healthiest way possible; emotions are something that you should never let bottle up. Talk to someone you trust. Hearing their opinion of the matter can help to broaden your thoughts and regain control.

Many people keep a journal to write down how they feel. Others engage in exercise to discharge their emotions. Others meditate in order to return to their tranquil state. Whatever activity suits you, find it and use it when emotions get high.

Look at the bigger picture

All happenings in our, both bad and good, serves a purpose in our lives. Being able to see past the moment strengthens your wisdom. You may not understand certain circumstances right away, but over time, you will see the bigger picture as the pieces of the puzzle fall into order. Even when in an emotionally upsetting time, trust that there is a reason that you will comprehend in time.

Replace your thoughts

Negatively fueled emotions create negative recurring thoughts that create cycles of negative patterns over time. When confronted with these emotions, force them out of your mind and replace them with more positive thoughts. Visualize the ideal ending playing out or think about someone or something that makes you happy.

Forgive your triggers

Triggers could be the ones you love the most; you're best friend(s), your family, yourself, etc. There will be times that you may feel a sudden wave of rage when people do things that annoy you or a self-loathing feeling when you remember back to the past when you could have done thing differently. The key to managing your emotions is to first, forgive. This allows you to detach from your jealousy, fury, and resentment. As you forgive, you will discover that disassociating yourself from these feelings will do you the best.

Every day we are constantly reminded of how strong and prominent our emotions are and the power they have. We are bound to take the wrong action from time to time and feel the wrong things. To avoid acting out, simply take a few steps back and calm your spirit that is heightened from outside forces. You will be grateful for mastering your emotions when it comes to building and strengthening meaningful relationships.

Using the Power of Mini Habits

Just after Christmas in the days ending 2016, I was reflecting on the year. I realized that I had tons of room to improve but always failed at keeping up with my New Year's resolutions. Instead, I decided that in 2017, I would explore other options.

On the 28th of December, I made the choice that I wanted to get back in shape. Previously, I hardly if ever exercised and had a consistent guilt about it. My goal was a 30-minute workout, realistic, right?

I found myself unmotivated, tired, and the guilt made me feel worthless. It wasn't until a few days later that I came across a small blog article about thinking the opposite of the ideas you are stuck on. The clear opposite of my 30-minute workout goal was chilling on the couch, stuffing my face with junk food, but my brain went to the idea of 'size.'

What if, instead of carrying that guilty feeling around all the time, I just performed one push-up? I know, right? How absurd of me to think that a single push-up would do anything to help me towards my goal.

What I found was a magical secret to unlocking my potential…when I found myself struggling with my bigger goals; I gave in and did a push-up. Since I was already down on the floor, I did a few more. Once I performed a few, my muscles felt warmed up and I decided to attempt a pull-up. As you can imagine, I did several more. And soon, I exercised for entire 30-minutes!

What Are Mini Habits?

Mini habits are just like they sound; you choose a habit you want to change and you shrink them down to stupidly small tasks.

For instance, if you want to start writing at least 1,000 words per day:

- Write 50 words per day

- Read two pages of a book per day

Easy, right? I could accomplish this in 10 to 20 minutes or so. You will find that once you start meeting this daily requirement, you will far exceed them faster than you would imagine.

What is *More* Essential than Your *Habits*?

You might be wondering how you can become more comfortable in your skin and be yourself in a cruel world with these so-called mini habits. Well, think about it; what is more important than the things you do each and every day? NOTHING. Habits are responsible for 45% of how we behave, making up the foundation of who we are and how happy we are in life.

The main reason people fail to change anything in their life, even the aspects they know need to change is because they never instill new habits. Why? Simply because in the past, they have tried to do way too much, all at once. If establishing a new habit requires you to have more willpower than you can muster, you are bound to be unsuccessful. If a habit requires less willpower, you are much more likely to succeed!

Benefits of Mini Habits

There are many additional benefits that come with utilizing mini habits in your everyday life. Here are a few:

- Consistent success breeds more success
- No more guilt
- Stronger productivity
- Formation of more positively impactful habits
- Generation of motivation

Chapter 5: Belittle anxiety with personal empowerment

Having a negative attitude towards life keeps us from being happy and impacts those that we interact daily with. Science has more than enough proof to show how being positive impacts your levels of happiness and terms of success. This is why making positivity a habit with the help of small changes can help you to drastically change your overall life and the mindset you have towards the world. The life you are living is a direct reflection of your overall attitude. It can be quite easy, almost too easy, to be cynical at the world and see it as a mess of injustice and tragedy, especially thanks to the media that we all spend many hours a day on.

Negativity is holding you back from really enjoying your life and has a great impact on your environment as well. The energy that people bring to the table, including you, is very contagious. One of the best things you can do in your life that is free of charge and simplistic is to offer your positive attitude. This is especially beneficial in a world that loves and craves negativity.

One of my favorite quotes of all time comes directly from the King of Pop, Michael Jackson: *"If you want to make the world a better place, take a look at yourself and make a change."*

As humans, we are creatures of habit. In this chapter, we will outline small but significant changes that can be made to form positive habits that can drastically change the overall mindset of your life around.

Smile

When asked who we think about most of the time, the most honest answer would probably have to be ourselves, right? This is natural, so don't feel guilty! It is good to hold ourselves accountable and take responsibility for ourselves.

But I want to challenge you to put yourself aside for at least one moment per day (I recommend striving for more) and make another person smile.

Think about making someone else happy and that warm feeling you get when you receive happiness. We don't realize how intense the impact of making someone smile can have on those around us. Plus, smiling costs nothing and positively works your facial muscles!

Focus on solutions, not problems

Embracing positivity doesn't mean you need to avoid issues, but rather it is learning how to reconstruct the way you criticize. Those that are positive create criticisms with the idea to improve something. If you are just going to point out the issues with people and in situations, then you should learn to place that effort instead into suggesting possible solutions. You will find that pointing out solutions makes everyone feel more positive than pointing out flaws.

Notice the rise, not just the downfall

Many of us are negative just by the simple fact that we dwell too much on the hate and violence that is in our daily media. But what we fail to notice is those that are rising up, showing compassion, and giving love to others. Those are the stories you should engulf yourself in. When you able to find modern-day heroes in everyday life, you naturally feel more hopeful, even in tough times.

Just breathe

Our emotions are connected to the way we breathe. Think about a time that you held your breath when you were in deep concentration or when you are upset or anxious. Our breath is dependent on how we feel, which means it also has the power to change our emotions too!

Fend off other's negativity

I'm sure you have gone to work cheerful and excited to take on the day ahead, but then your co-worker ruins that happy-go-lucky mood of yours with their complaints about every little thing, from the weather to other employees, to their weekend, etc.

It is natural to find yourself agreeing to what others are saying, especially if you like to avoid conflict. But you are initially allowing yourself to drown in their pool of negative emotions. Don't fall into this trap.

Conflict may arise, but I challenge you to not validate the complaints of a friend, family member, or co-worker next time they are going about on a complaint-spree. They are less likely to be negative in the future if they have fewer people to complain to.

Switch the "*I have to*" mindset with "*I get to*"

I am sure you often fail to notice how many times we tell ourselves that we have to go and do something.

- "I have to go to work."
- "I have to go to the store."
- "I have to pay rent."
- "I have to mow the lawn."

You get the picture. But watch what happens when you swap the word have with the word get.

- "I get to go to work."
- "I get to go to the store."
- "I get to pay rent."
- "I get to mow the lawn."

See the change in attitude there? It goes from needing to fulfill those obligations to be grateful that you have those things to do in your life. This means:

- You have a job to go to
- You have enough money to support yourself and your family to provide a healthy meal
- You have a roof over your head
- You have a nice yard

When you make this simple change, you will begin to feel the warmth of happiness snuggle you like the cold blanket of stress falls away.

Describe your life positively

The choice of vocabulary we use has much more power over our lives than we realize. How you discuss your life is essential to harnessing positivity since your mind hears what you spew out loud.

When you describe your life as boring, busy, chaotic, and/or mundane, this is exactly how you will continue to perceive it and it will directly affect both your mental and physical health.

Instead, if you describe your life as involved, lively, familiar, simple, etc., you will begin to see changes in your overall perspective and you will find more joy in the way you choose to mold your entire life.

Master rejection

You will need to learn to become good at being rejected. The fact of the matter is, rejection is a skill. Instead of viewing failed interviews and broken hearts as failures, see them as opportunities for practice to ensure you are ready for what is to come next. Even if you try to avoid it, rejection is inevitable. Don't allow it to harden you from the inside out.

Rethink challenges

Stop picturing your life being scattered with dead-end signs and view all your failings as opportunities to re-direct. There are little to no things in life that we have 100-percent control over. When you let uncontrollable experiences take over your life, you will literally turn into mush.

What you can control is the amount of effort you put into things without an ounce of regret doing them! When you are able to have fun taking on challenges, you are embracing adventure and the unknown, which allows you much more room to grow, learn and win in the future.

Write in a gratitude journal

There are bound to be days where just one situation can derail the entire day, whether it be an interaction that is not so pleasant or something that happens the night before the day ahead, our mind clings to these negative aspects of the day.

I am sure you have read on multiple sites about how keeping a gratitude journal is beneficial. If you are anything like me, I thought this was total rubbish that is until I started doing it. I challenged myself to write down at least five things that I was truly grateful for each and every day. Scientifically, expressing gratitude is linked to happiness and reducing stress.

I challenge you to begin jotting down things you appreciate and are grateful for each day. Even on terrible days, there is something to be blessed about!

Chapter 6: Everyday techniques to fend off anxiety

Despite the toll that anxiety and its symptoms can have on everyday life and fulfillment, in today's world there are many different techniques and methods you can learn to incorporate into your everyday routine that help you to control and possibly even eliminate anxiety from your life. Each section of this chapter will be dedicated to a specific genre of techniques that anyone has the ability to learn!

Visualization and Anxiety

Seeing *is* believing, which is a key secret to how entrepreneurs and well-known people in society stand out and achieve success and fulfill their dreams. *Visualization is the simple use of imagination through mental imagery to help form visions of what we want in our lives and how we can make them a reality.*

There are two main kinds of visualization:

Pragmatic Visualization represents a set of days that helps to gain new ideas and interpret what it says/means to them. It helps those understand structures that lie within a set of data.

Artistic Visualization is similar to pragmatic in that it utilizes visuals to convey information but in a different sense. It is used to show people that data is being monitored carefully and shows particular aspects of data that is connected to one another to depict an entire idea.

So, how does learning about these two kinds of visualization help you in your quest to decrease anxiety? Well, visual techniques help to drastically overcome symptoms of anxiety. When the two types are combined, visualization is powerful in obtaining and staying in a calmer state of mind.

When it comes to anxiety, visualization requires one to picture themselves in a safe, peaceful and/or tranquil environment. Anywhere that makes you happier is where you should be imagining yourself during visualization exercises. It does sound pretty funny at first glance, but trust me when I say there is something about being able to transport your mind to somewhere mentally tranquil. Not only will your mind thank you but your body will too, for it becomes much more relaxed and stress-free when performing these practices. Visualization gives people something to distract themselves from the current world that surrounds them.

Why You Should Be Using Visualization

Beyond visualization itself, you can literally view the best of life from the comfort of your own couch. This chapter will showcase the benefits that come with the dedicated practice of learning and incorporating ways of visualization into your everyday life.

- **Improved quality of relationships** – The positive outcomes of utilizing visualization doesn't just end within yourself. Since you are developing a better mindset that aids in your views and beliefs, those around you will like and appreciate the more confident, positive you!

- **Boosts your mood** – When one practices the methods of visualization, they naturally experience a sort of joy that is quite unexplainable to some. Once you finish one of these sessions successfully, you will more than likely feel boastfully happy, calm and relaxed.

- **Relieves stress** – Practicing the ways of visualization naturally causes one to be able to relax. It has a way of quieting the mind to be able to think happier, more positive thoughts which tone down loads of stress that pile on our shoulders almost on a daily basis.

- **Strengthens the immune system** – Thanks to all that dialing down of stress and things that fuel stress, your body is better able to fight off sickness which makes you physically better, longer. This also helps in aiding anxiety because you are not constantly worrying about getting ill all the time as well.

- **Ability to learn new things quicker** – When the mind is in a calmer state, it is able to pick up and grasp new concepts much easier than when it is bogged down with so many negative thoughts and emotions.

- **Able to cope with the feeling of nervousness** – When you take time out of your day to practice visualization, you are initially settling all those negative feelings that you may have about yourself and what others may think of you as well. This immensely helps individuals who are naturally more nervous combat that feeling, which leaves room to try and experiment with new things and ideas. Imagine yourself in a great looking outfit giving that inevitable speech that is due soon. Then imagine an applauding audience. It is quite the confidence booster!

- **Builds stronger concentration skills** – Visualization makes room for your mind to do other tasks efficiently by spring cleaning negative thoughts, feelings, emotions, and past experiences. This doesn't mean it is responsible for getting rid of them 100%, but it helps one to be able to cope and bring down those bad levels to make room for productivity.

- **Assists in overcoming recurring issues** – When the weight of your entire world is upon your shoulders, it is no wonder that we begin to believe that our lives were just made to be a laughing-stalk to some because of how life's unlucky events have left us feeling. This can lead to long-term problems and beliefs. Visualization combats these two things.

- **Can give you a spark of inspiration** – During your sessions, if your mind always veers to one idea in particular, perhaps it is time to take initiative and proceed with the steps in achieving it! Visualizing doing something can directly inspire you to do as such.

- **Makes one more creative** – Visualization not only takes concentration but also a truckload of creativity as well. If you are going to picture something in detail and add the other four senses to that visual, you have to really want to mold it into reality. We all have creative bones in our bodies. Visualization just brings them out more, honing that skill and letting it shine.

- **No boundaries** – As I have mentioned before, when it comes to visualization, practice makes perfect. Just like with any newly acquired skill, one must learn to hone its practice to be able to tweak it when needed and use it to their utmost advantage. With certain visualization techniques, you can literally picture yourself doing something that would otherwise be usually hard to achieve. With those images in mind, you then have a good idea what you must do to actually and realistically accomplish that image you had in your head during a visualization session. This method knows no bounds!

- **Method of practice and rehearsal** – Believe it or not, visualization can be a way to practice your favorite sport or nail that upcoming work pitch that you have been reciting and memorizing for days. Picturing yourself doing or performing something is just as effective as actually completing the task at hand. Utilizing visualization with real, physical practice can get you to honing that skill or memorizing things much quicker.

- **Picture yourself getting stronger and healthier** – Sounds unbelievable, but if you are sick, seeing yourself get better will have the result of getting healthier, sooner. Visualization reduces stress and relaxes your mind, which also assists in healing your body of sickness or physical injury as well. This allows your body to function at its full capacity. You would be surprised what our bodies could accomplish in a day's work if we treated them more like the temples they are and should always be. It is safe to say we take our physical presence for granted most days. And it tends to show more often than not!

- **Gives us joy** – Many people who practice the ways of visualization tend to picture something that brings them happiness. We almost are never quite in the right place or time in our lives to always have what we want and that is okay! But that doesn't mean we shouldn't get the luxury of seeing it for ourselves, right? Picturing a goal or what we want the most from life can bring us quite a load of temporary happiness if one wants to view it that way. Why temporary? If you can picture it, you can eventually and more than likely make it happen in your future, which is why visualization can be a great motivator.

Aspects of Successful Visualization Practices

There are three aspects to successfully become one with visualization:

- **Practice** – Learning the ways of visualization may actually be more stressful and frustrating for beginners because it is not a practice we are naturally keen to perform. Those that start practicing visualization have a false sense of what the experience is supposed to feel like and have false expectations about the outcome. This inhibits the practice from really taking effect. Visualization is something that has to be practiced daily to work for you long-term. If practiced the right way, it will eventually become second nature to you but only if you really dedicate yourself to learning its ways and practicing it every day until you have it down pat.

- **Utilizes ALL the senses** – Visualization doesn't just use your sense of how a certain peaceful place appears to you in your mind. You have to imagine what your safe space smells, tastes sounds and feels like as well. The more detailed you are in regards to your senses, the better visualization you will have and the more relaxed you can potentially become.

- **Actions** – All human beings experience mental barriers that keep them from being happy and the process of practicing and performing visualization is not excluded from this. Even for visualizing experts, bad thoughts from the course of one's day can inhibit one from getting a clear vision of their safe haven. You have to find a way to release and/or transform those bad thoughts and feelings into something that you can tangibly get rid of.

Forms of Visualization for Anxiety

Visualization is a skill that can be utilized to obtain a better life, especially for those that suffer from an anxiety disorder. Now, we will talk about techniques in the visualization world. Although all of these are not for everyone, try them out and see what works for you.

Meditation

Meditation is a superb form of apathetic visualization that can lead to very powerful results. Visualizing through means of meditation is more of an outgrowth than the main focus. When you begin to incorporate meditation sessions into your everyday routine, you will gradually be opening the door to your inner self, which will then lead you to be able to visualize more clearly and easily.

The more experience you have with meditation, the smoother sessions become and the more you get to see and take away from your visions. It is important not to become frustrated with yourself or discouraged from continuing to practice meditation if you are just starting out.

The whole point of meditation is to empty your brain of thoughts and feelings and to let your mind wander to wherever it wants to go. A vital component of meditation is breathing. Learn to focus on how you take in and let out breaths of air. Let your mind veer off to wherever its little heart desires. Once you begin to practice this technique more often, it will become easier and faster to exhaust your mind of concerns or other worries and let other things come in and explore. It will become second nature for you to sit down, relax and get into a clear state of mind so that you can visualize to your contentment.

Meditation makes way for things that you never thought were actually within you. Once you rid your brainwaves of all that noise from the course of your day, thoughts occur at their own pace.

Altered Memory Visualization

This visualization technique targets past memories and learning how to change them to a more positive standpoint. For those with anxiety about things that stem from their past, this is especially helpful in obtaining a brighter state of mind. This technique is one to utilize if you are one that holds on to past anger and resentment from particular situations that you finally want to rid yourself of.

No one can change the past, but you can teach your brain how it views these past scenarios in your mind. Get into a calmed state and visualize the scenario that you wish had a different outcome. Restore things said that were fueled by anger with comments that are controlled and peaceful. This does take some time and you may have to revisit this scene in your head multiple times to nail the outcome that you wish had resulted from the past situation. It is recommended to not do this day upon day in a row, but rather space out revisiting the scene.

Over time, your brain will begin to only recall what YOU have recreated, making a once painful or uncomfortable situation fade away in memory. Try to imagine little cubicle offices in each major section of your brain. In this instance, I like to picture a little office guy that is in charge of just the bad memories. During these sessions, you are instructing him on how to rewrite particular events that have occurred in the past and once they are rewritten the way you once anticipated them to play out, this office dude can start to shred your memories of these occurrences.

Receptive Visualization

This technique is much like viewing a movie inside your head, but you are the director of the scenes within this movie. Get yourself to a quiet space, lie back, get comfortable and close your eyes. Focus on building the scene in which you want to see acted out in your mind.

Once a clear backdrop and scenery is within your mind, place people, noises, smells and sounds within your scene of this movie. It is best to slowly build your way up to the actual scene until you are comfortable and content with it, then it is time for action! Focus on feeling involved within this scene of your "movie."

Treasure Map

This visualization technique not only uses mental fundamentals but also physical components as well. You will need to have an idea of what you want to visualize before getting to the nitty-gritty of performing this method. Start by using your art skills to draw out some type of physical representation of the components you need to achieve in order to reach your ultimate goal.

For example, perhaps you have an upcoming test that you want to get a great grade on. Draw out a building symbolizes a school, a book that you will need to use to study for this test and then a representation of yourself. Try to make your drawing detailed, but do not worry about the maturity of your art abilities too much here. It is not the drawings themselves that are important, but rather what you are imagining WHILE sketching them out.

As you draw out your "map to success", your mind is actually visualizing ways that will get you to where you want to be. Patience is a key with this particular technique, for it does take a bit of time to truly become completely mentally occupied in this exercise. It is crucial to take your notepad and pen to a quiet space and to not be around anything distracting such as a radio, television, people or phones.

How to Design Your Own "Safe Space"

Safe places or spaces are a mind's sanctuary, created for the purpose of retreat if one needs a mental location to be able to visualize or hone their meditative state and reduce stress. Creating one of these is kind of like personalizing a physical space in your home. You want to do anything to truly make it YOURS.

It can be anything from a room inside an imaginary home, a room in your realistic home that you want to visualize differently, the beach, a comforting outdoorsy area, etc. As you meditate or relax and begin to dive deeper into your imagery or visualization session, this is the place you imagine you want to go. It is anywhere that you wish to return to time after time, so put some effort and thought into where you will always find comfort in mentally retreating to.

- **Brainstorm** – The goal is to develop a place that you feel calm, content and happy within, no matter the reason that you retreat to it. If you have difficulty seeking out such a place, start by looking through art, magazines, books, old photographs, etc. Always lean towards ideas that burst with positivity for you.

- Are you more apt to feel calmer in an outdoor/natural setting or do you feel better within the walls of some type of structure?

- Are there pieces of writing such as within books, poems of stories that make you feel at ease?

- Do you feel more comforted by populated areas or tranquil areas?

- **Think of a time where you felt happy and safe** – Memories are the best areas to seek things that bring joy to you. Think back to memories that you were happy, content, playful, peaceful, etc. Write these down in detail. It could be literally anywhere, as long as it brought contentment to you.

  - Where did this memory occur?
  - How old were you?
  - Why did this memory make you happy?
  - Who was with you within this memory?

- **Create various rooms** – Your safe space does not necessarily have to be just 2D, one room vision. It can have various sections, compartments or rooms within it. This allows you to trek to different areas throughout your visualization sessions. This also allows one the ability to be able to compartmentalize issues and deal with them one part at a time.

  - *Fill your space with cherished people* – There are many individuals that would rather be alone while in their safe place, while others prefer the company of their favorite people. Imagine who makes you happy and during the course of a visualization session, imagine greeting them and welcoming them into your safe space. This also goes for people in your life that may have passed away that you miss and wish to see. Having conversations with them and asking for advice could make a world of difference!

- *Utilize ALL your senses* – Seeing is believing, but visions of your safe place are a lot more believable and turn in better results if you learn to engage all your senses while within them. Engulf yourself in tastes, sounds smells and how things feel between your fingers and toes and against your skin. It will enhance your visualization experience ten-fold.

- *Write out all the details* – Once you have taken the dedicated time to develop and build your safe place, write down all the tiniest details that you can remember. Writing in a lot of detail can assist you in returning to that place in your mind easier and more efficiently. Some individuals even videotape, sculpt, draw or paint out their descriptions for safekeeping for future use.

    - Are there animals or people?
    - What do you feel?
    - How small or big is your space?
    - What colors?
    - What surrounds you?
    - What is the ultimate backdrop or setting?

- **Visualize positive results** – The main rule of thumb for visualization is imagining situations acted out in positive manners. This involves a heavy amount of thinking happily and setting up a content scene. Imaging positive outcomes are really just a more in-depth version of regular run-of-the-mill positive thinking.

Developing Anxiety Routines

Anxiety routines are any type of daily routine that you use to calm yourself down in stressful situations and that leaves you feeling physical, mental or emotionally distressed. These routines are meant to help you bounce back from the depths of your own thoughts and live a life full of more passion and fulfillment.

This means it is very crucial to choose routines that not only suit you but are healthy, too. Life runs smoother when you have a routine to fulfill those nasty little voices in your head or when you feel like you may make a bad choice because of your anxiety symptoms. Sadly, some people choose unhealthy habitual routines that not only push them back into a negative state but may even provoke symptoms of anxiety and make them worse.

These bad routines could be anything from drug use, both illegal and prescription, large consumption of alcohol or heavy smoking of cigarettes, etc. You get the picture. Creating an anxiety routine for yourself should not include things that will cause you greater harm in the long run. Honestly, habits like those stated above are only going to make your symptoms worse.

As human beings, we are automatically wired to detect any sort of negative energy that may cause us harm. Anxiety becomes so bad within certain people simply because our bodies do not quite know the difference between stressful triggers that are actually harmless to us versus actual, life-threatening aspects that may be sprung upon us.

Our bodies are made to react to protect ourselves. This is why being mentally prepared for the day that lies ahead of you is so crucial, especially for anxiety sufferers. It is important to back up our thoughts with an extra layer of positivity to promote a sense of safety and well-being. This is much easier said than done, especially when life may not have been a very good friend to you as of late. But being able to mentally develop a positive sense of self is the first step in creating daily routines that help pave your way to a successful life to live and your future.

Routines to Decrease Anxiety

With the right amount of inspiration, the first day or two of adding a new routine to your life can be exciting. You know you are making a positive change that will hopefully help you feel better about yourself and the life you live. However, self-care routines can be a hard thing to manage and utilize on a regular basis once the newness of acting upon it wears off.

Anxiety can leave some sufferers so dismayed by anxious or sad thoughts that they want nothing more than to do away with anything that resonates positive energy. But this is the exact opposite of fighting for yourself and your happiness. Everyone has their bad days and moments and by all means, you are allowed to have and live those. But it is important not to stay tucked away in them for long periods of time.

Developing and executing specific daily routines that you are comfortable with gives those a step by step plan for the day and keeps you prepared for situations or other anxiety triggers from leaping out and mugging you of your happiness. Routines, kind of like exercise, are things we practice daily to keep us in shape, but anxious routines keep our minds in check. You never know when something will catch you off guard, when a person may ask you something that is bothersome or when a debilitating symptom of anxiety will hit you throughout the course of the day. It is better to be prepared than not to be, right?

The Importance of a Balanced Morning Routine

Many functions within routines do them absolutely no good. When the alarm goes off, they tend to hit snooze a few times. When they finally decide to open their eyes, they automatically reach for their phones and look at updates on social media. Many people are already let down by the fact no one messaged them or liked their posts throughout the night.

When their feet finally touch the floor to stand up out of bed, they are already on a path to a negative, self-destructing day. They take a quick shower, down a bowl of cereal and chug a cup of coffee and get to their day job...what is the point?

This lack of routine is non-beneficial. We see our unstructured lives as having no real purpose, which results in a lack of inner peace. We are destroying our happiness without realizing it!

Benefits of a Morning Routine

Creating a morning routine is not only a big part in relieving anxiety, but it also boosts productivity, brings out your inner positivity, helps you to develop and successfully sustain good relationships, as well as being a big reducer of negativities. Morning routines alone have been shown to be the best strategy for reducing stress and relieving those pesky symptoms of anxiety, no matter how long they have resided within you.

Morning routines keep you consciously aware and more grounded throughout the day. In fact, many who were once stubborn and did not want to incorporate a daily routine were eventually surprised at how much better they felt each and every morning. Anxiety levels dropped and confidence and happiness levels substantially rose. A morning routine can literally reduce your anxiety by as much as sixty percent!

Steps to Include in Your Morning Routine

When you **wake up earlier,** you know that you have plenty of time to get up and get ready for your day, which aids in decreased stress levels. If there is adrenaline pumping throughout your body as you rush around to head out the door, it sticks with you for the rest of the day.

Sounds like a waste of time, but **making your bed each morning** is a powerful task that helps you gain the momentum you need to get pumped for the day ahead. For those that suffer from anxiety and depression, making the bed is simple but can make a huge difference because you know you have completed *one* task if not anything else.

Meditation and prayer is a subject with many critics. People view meditation as an act performed only by spiritual individuals. Practicing mindfulness daily has positive side effects that can trigger feel-good hormones in the brains that aid in reducing levels of stress, anxiety and even depression.

Mixing meditation and prayer within your morning routine can be quite vitalizing, giving clarity to your life and your decisions. If you wish to learn more about the power behind the act of prayer, it will be covered in the following chapter The Empowerment of Prayer.

Taking an ice cold shower in the mornings has been proven to provide the human body with a great number of benefits. Cold exposure, also known as cold shower therapy, is nothing new. Our ancestors utilized it as a remedy to treat mental ailments. Showering in cold water provides the body with adequate circulation and tones the skin nicely.

The cold feeling kicks positive responses throughout the body into overdrive. It accelerates the repairing of cells, which reduces inflammation, pain, and speeds up our metabolic processes. The icy waters help lower negative levels that depression and anxiety can hover over us. Standing under the cold water for just a couple minutes can yield you these benefits.

Substitute your breakfast with coffee or tea to bump up energy levels and replace your usual breakfast eats. This is not recommended for absolutely everyone, but if you are trying to find ways to keep hunger away for the first portion of your day, give it a shot!

Learn how to **utilize a journal** to make "morning pages" as part of your routine in the mornings. This is my personal favorite way to "mind dump" any curious or troubling thoughts you had during the previous day and the night before, as well as random ideas that pop into your mind. I write in my journal after taking a shower, since great ideas tend to spring during those few minutes. When you are able to write down all the negative feelings on paper, you can then get through the day with a clearer state of mind.

Practice gratitude by jotting down things you would miss if they were no longer in your life, such as objects, people, etc. into your morning pages.

To start the day on a positive note, **jot down what you are looking forward** to that day. This tells our brains to look up, think up and be bright and helps to relieve anxiety.

Write down your intentions at the beginning of each day, no matter how corny they may sound, such as *"I will choose to be consciously present today."*

Write out important tasks that you wish to achieve during the day to ensure you will feel prepared and have a fulfilling plan. This will ease your mind so that you can develop a clear path of action to achieving that days' goals.

I know I have mentioned writing a lot, but like I said before it is a powerful tool. Every morning our brains are ready to go and on high alert, so it is good to have a well-thought-out plan of action.

Write down at least three to five of the most important tasks that you have to complete. Focus on ones that stress you out just thinking about them. Then, ask yourself the following questions about the tasks you have jotted out so that you can prioritize them accordingly:

- Which tasks will help me inch closer to achieving my main goal?

- What task do I have the most fearful anxious thoughts about?

- Which tasks have the potential to cancel out others if done successfully?

Spend 90 minutes every day working towards accomplishing your priorities. Targeting your main goals during the morning hours help you to get them accomplished productively.

Other Morning Methods to Relieve Anxiety

Play uplifting music to ensure an upbeat, positive mood. Create a playlist to play throughout your morning routine. Make your phone's alarm tone a good song to wake up to. You would be surprised at what a difference this effortless step takes.

Spend time with a pet(s) to help raise your dopamine and serotonin levels, resulting in lessened anxiety and depression. Pets also motivate us to climb out of bed and give us the initiative to take on the day, even when our anxiety tries to get the best of us. Adding them to your morning routine is a bonus for not only you but for your pet's well-being too!

Change your scenery in simple ways; Go outside, take a walk. Visit your favorite café and grab a coffee. Go out with a friend. The longer you dwell in a space that sucks away happiness, the worse you will feel.

Interactions with the outside world can be enough to distract you from your anxious habits. This is another reason routines are so important in aiding anxiety. Avoiding responsibilities can actually damage you mentally more than you realize. It is good to get your attention off the darkness of life that resides inside your head. It only makes your anxiety worse when you sit around and obsess over it.

Coping with anxiety and its symptoms can lead to a life of great discomfort. Having some type of structure in the form of routines can be quite crucial to one's success in living a happy, go-lucky life. The next few chapters will cover other types of routines in detail that can help relieve and maybe even make your symptoms disappear for good! It is all about you to initiate making the change.

Chapter 7: Transforming Your anxiety for a better life

If you are feeling anxious or depressed about your future and are allowing negative thoughts to get the best of you and dampen your motivation for success, then learning to use anxiety to your advantage is a must.

Personally, I have learned to *choose* to view my anxiety has a valuable asset that yields me to lead a more authentic life. I live empathetically, for my anxiety has made me a vulnerable person and thus, helped me deepen my life's relationships.

Having anxiety just means I am not mellow enough to take things for granted in life, therefore, making life a richer experience all the way around. In fact, there are a few inspirational ways that anxiety has helped me to elevate my life:

- Got me actively involved in personal development
- Taught me how to think in the present and act now
- Got me reading more books and discover how it heals the mind
- Started me on tracking my success and not just on failure
- Taught me how to make a positive game out of my life
- Assisted me to take control over my life
- Reconnected me to the habit of learning new things every day
- Showed me the power of meditation and visualization
- Allowed me to see that I am not the only one in my life that suffers from degrees of anxiety
- Has taught me to be a more actively vulnerable person

Using Anxiety to Your Advantage

Believe it or not, anxiety can be used for good and can be a powerful force in motivating yourself to achieve your desires. Using stress to add momentum to your life is constructive, instead of allowing it to deconstruct our lives.

Redefining danger

You must learn to see anxiety differently; anxiety, before our brains get a hold of it and dwell, is just a warning sign used for our survival. At this point, you are allowing anxiety to make you feel panicked. But even when that warning sign lights up, it doesn't mean you are in danger. You must save this energy for when you really need to make quick decisions.

Create a list of less to most dangerous to help identify a good spectrum of threats. With that comparison, you will be able to see what "dangerous" situations are safe and which ones are frightening.

Channel your stress properly

Diamonds don't grow from trees; they are coals that turn into something more beautiful through pressure. Channeling stress positively into energy for motivation does take time and can be physically and emotionally draining. But instead of allowing negative thoughts take hold of you and send you down that same spiraling hole of anxiety, look at the situation before you differently; view it as your time to *shine*! When negativity starts to manifest in your mind, challenge those thoughts. When you challenge them, you will find that the negativity in them is totally empty in the first place.

Stop trying to do your best

There are two kinds of people: those that do their best and those that can *do better*. However, those that strive to do their best constantly are the ones that end up emotionally drained than those who do better. Why? Because when you do your best, you are settling. When you strive to *do better*, you accept that you are not doing as good as you know you can. For anxiety sufferers, what they do isn't good enough for them. They either drown in their shortcomings or have learned to take the opportunity to improve themselves.

In those with anxiety, underestimation is a common cognitive distortion. When we tell ourselves that we can do better, we know how to reject our deficiencies and go out of their way to prove themselves wrong.

Chapter 8: Battling anxiety like a true warrior

"The only thing we have to fear is fear itself."

- *President Theodore Roosevelt*

Marines, SEALs, and Special Forces have no choice but to face life-threatening danger head-on regularly. The fact is, if they do get caught up in fear, they are more likely to lose their lives. While many of us will thankfully never have to face these experiences, why aren't we using the fear-crushing tactics that they use in our own personal lives?

Spend time preparing

If you are worried about a work presentation, stressing over a job interview, or freaking out about the upcoming rap battle that might help you move out of your mom's house, then stop, prepare, and practice instead of sitting around. The key is to lose yourself in the moment, which you to by devoting a ton of energy into preparing for what you are worried about. Spend 75% preparing and 25% for the actual event.

SEALs are able to erase fear by practicing upcoming mission until they feel naturally confident. When the unknown becomes more known to them, they don't have to lie to themselves about the risks, but instead put themselves in a better position to handle the unknown, which develops confidence.

Learn to *manage* fear

One of the best ways to deal with fear is to laugh about it. What? You read that right! Laughter lets you know that things are going to be okay and work out. Don't worry; there is evidence to back this theory up. A study by Stanford University showed that those that were trained to make jokes to respond to negative images. This is a much healthier way to deal with fear. The world is an inevitably twisted place, so seeing the funnier side of things makes it easier to deal with.

Breathe

When your heart is beating from your chest, your joints turn into Jell-O, and sweat is pouring off your face, then the best thing you can do to calm the physical manifestations of fear derived from anxiety is to breathe.

That simple? YES. By just inhaling for four seconds and exhaling for four seconds, SEALs can calm their nervous systems and maintain control of their natural biological responses to fear.

You are essentially bending your body's software to better control the hardware. In other words, you are giving yourself a pretty bomb superpower! Breathing helps the body go from the fight-or-flight response of the sympathetic nervous system to the relaxed response of the parasympathetic nervous system.

Tactical breathing used by Navy SEALS for performance just prior to a tense situation or during a workout:

Breathe through the nose. It's very important to breathe through your nose since breathing through the nose stimulates nerve cells that exist behind sternum near the spine that triggers the parasympathetic nervous system. Anxiety is a sympathetic response and parasympathetic counteracts that. This calms your body, which then calms your mind.

1. Relaxed sitting position and right handle on the belly.

2. Activate the breath by pushing belly out and then inhale deeply for a count of four. Inhale to the belly. This pulls breath deep into the lungs. Exhale through the nose for a count of four, pulling the belly button toward the spine. Repeat this three times.

3. Now breathe in through belly and diaphragm for a count of four, again inhaling into your belly and this time lifting your chest. Again, exhale

for a count of four so that your rib cage falls and your belly button pulls toward your spine. Repeat three times.

4. Next, use the same technique, this time inhaling for a count of four through the belly, diaphragm and your chest, with a slight raise of shoulders for inhaling. Exhale for a count of four three the chest, diaphragm, and then the belly. Repeat three times, eventually working your breaths up to eight counts.

Next, box breathing is a technique used by the U.S. Navy SEALS to maintain focus and to calm nervous system after a tense situation, such as combat, an intense workout or anytime the desire is to center and focus.

Trains for diaphragmic breathing or deep breathing. Relaxes the whole system and provides oxygen to the brain to focus better. Improves energy. It can also be used by you to regain your sense of balance, concentration, and relaxation and can be practiced at any time. Use the same technique as tactical breathing but you use a five-count hold between breaths.

1. Get in a relaxed sitting position
2. Inhale deeply through the nose for five seconds
3. Hold the air in your lungs for five seconds
4. Exhale for five seconds, releasing all the air from your lungs
5. Hold your lungs empty for five seconds
6. Repeat for five minutes, or as long as you feel necessary

Don't keep things bottled up

Fear is just like terrible liquor; it sucks when you drink it and has negative effects that last a long time, which is why it is important to deal with it before and after the fact.

Talking about scary experiences helps soldiers locate the meaning behind it all. This communication allows them to process what they have been through positively and helps them to create closer relationships with their mates. Scared? Admit it to a friend. Hearing it out loud can help you pull it out, confront it, and deal with it.

Overpower that inner nagging voice

We are all aware of the inner chatter that occurs in our mind on a daily basis. In fact, our inner voice can be really negative the majority of the time. Wouldn't it be cool to have an inner monologue that reminds us how confident and awesome we are? Wouldn't it be great to have an inner motivational speaker to get us through tough times?

Well, you can. In times of stress, our brains are wired to create self-talk that can increase our feelings of fear. As a soldier, they are expected to fight against their inner self-talk and focus on positive portions of experiences. With practice, they are easily able to ignore or even erase the negativity their brains are throwing at them. So, you can do the same in your own life.

Fear and anxiety thrive when we imagine the worst. We developed imagination to be able to project into the future so we can plan ahead. However, a side effect of being able to imagine possible positive futures is being able to imagine things going wrong. A bit of this is useful; after all, there really might be muggers or loan sharks. But uncontrolled imagination is a testing ground for anxiety and fear that can spoil otherwise happy lives.

Some people misuse their imagination chronically and so suffer much more anxiety than those who either future-project their imaginations constructively or who don't tend to think about the future much at all. Anxious, chronic worriers tend to misuse their imaginations to the extent that upcoming events feel like catastrophes waiting to happen. No wonder whole lives can be blighted by fear and anxiety.

Think of the worst-case scenario

No matter what you are afraid of, you always have the opportunity to avoid it for the rest of your life. However, soldiers don't get that choice. They face similar situations time and time again that scare them. To ensure fear doesn't overrule them, they simulate stressful scenarios and try to experience the emotions with them as well.

Instead of thinking happy thoughts and ignoring what you are afraid of, start looking at the worst things that can possibly happen. When you are able to picture the worst fear and stay within an emotional experience instead of pushing yourself out of it, your mind tends to get over the fear naturally.

Reframe your mindset

Reframe you definition of symptoms. Reframe the symptoms of anxiety - give them a different meaning. Those sweaty palms, racing heart, and lightheadedness can mean a panic attack or they can mean the most exciting and fun adventure of your life! Your body doesn't know the difference and it is just doing what it does by nature, but you can choose how you define that sudden rush. Don't believe me?

How do you think those adrenaline junkies dives off cliffs, jump motorcycles or swim with sharks? Their definition of what we call fear is definitely different. They still experience the same potent chemicals coursing through their body, but the sensations have a different meaning to them. What you experience as fear, dread and near death can be defined as thrilling, exciting, and aliveness to someone else.

The beautiful thing about consistently and purposely redefining these symptoms is you can actually rewire your brain. This leads us to neuroplasticity.

Neuroplasticity

Neuroplasticity occurs with changes in behavior, thinking, and emotions. With conscious practice, we can alter our neural pathways to move naturally towards our desired emotions, such as being thankful, calm, and happy and away from anger, stress, and panic.

As you choose to respond with positive emotion, you can strengthen the neural pathways to the desired emotions. As you make more neural connections over time to your desired emotion, the pathways to the negative reactions eventually become weaker and scrambled. This even works while using mental rehearsals of the situation and practicing your desired response.

Remember, this can also work in reverse. If you have a habitual response to circumstances, such as being angry in a traffic jam and you repeat these responses over and over in a high state of emotion, you will strengthen the neural pathways towards the emotion of anger in that situation. The masters over the centuries who taught positive thinking and faith may have actually been on to something and now we can prove it scientifically.

Get moving

Exercise is usually associated with weight loss, improved physical health, and a stronger immune system. But the benefits of exercise can expand much more. Exercise is just as important for your mental fitness as it is your physical health. Aerobic activity promotes the release of endorphins that are released in the brain and act as painkillers, which also help to increase a sense of well-being. Endorphins also improve energy levels, provide a better night's sleep, elevate your mood and provide anti-anxiety effects. Exercise also takes your mind off of your worries and breaks the cycle of negative thoughts that contribute to anxiety.

It is recommended to perform 30 minutes or more of exercise five days a week to have a significant impact on anxiety symptoms. You don't need a formal exercise program at the gym to experience these benefits. Light physical activity has been shown to have the same effects, including gardening, housework, washing the car and walking around the block. These can be done in small intervals throughout the day.

It's more important to do some sort of physical activity on a consistent basis than to aim for something that is not sustainable. Be realistic and if you need to start with smaller goals, do so. This is all about taking care of yourself in a way that works for you.

The single, most important natural tool you can use to beat anxiety is regular exercise. It sounds cliché, but the truth is that exercise affects the mind and body in ways that science is still discovering.

There is a reason that anxiety prevalence has grown with our increasingly inactive lifestyles. Jogging every day can make a world of difference in how you deal with stress, how your anxiety symptoms manifest, and how you regulate your mood.

The best methods of exercise to combat anxiety are:

- **Running** releases feel-good hormones that have exponential mental health benefits. It can help you fall asleep faster, improve memory, lower stress levels, and protects against developing depression.

- **Hiking** in a wooded or hilly location has natural calming effects on the brain. Being around plants and Earthly sights helps to reduce anxiety thanks to the chemicals plants emit. Plus, being out in nature is great for your health and memory function.

- **Yoga,** a lot like meditation, has been found to significantly reduce anxiety and other neurotic symptoms that can lead to irritability and depression. It not only strengthens your core but helps you to focus on breathing, which is the key to relaxing the mind and combating anxiety.

Chapter 9: Rediscovering yourself after hurricane anxiety

Those that live with and through the darkness of anxiety can find themselves waking up each day unhappy. Life is short and there comes a time where re-evaluating your life in order to revamp parts of it to ensure your happiness and fulfillment.

We all get lost in life from time to time. We forget old passions we had, give up interest in pursuit of something else, etc. But it is never too late to rediscover what makes you great and what makes you feel truly alive.

When were you the *happiest?*

Take a moment to remember when you were the most content with your life. In high school? College? Before marriage, family, and kids? When you began your family? Started your business? Pursued a new hobby?

No one peaks at the same time or levels in their lives. The key to regaining contentment is not to think of those fond times as "the past", but to figure out how to find that feeling of happiness again where you currently are in your life. How can you re-incorporate those things that brought you joy in the life you are living now?

What makes you *unhappy?*

What makes your blood pressure shoot through the roof? Figuring out the things that push your last buttons is just as important as knowing what helps you keep a positive outlook. When you are able to clearly point out the toxic influences, you will be better able to erase them and develop better, healthier ways of living. We tend to hold onto things from the past that has negative impacts on our current lives. What grudges are you holding onto? These are toxic and are keeping you from being your best self! No matter what it is, from a toxic ex-partner to a job that drains you, cutting these negative influences will allow you ample space to grow in a positive direction.

Write!

When negative thoughts are constantly bouncing around the brain, it can be very easy to become overwhelmed. We tend to forget how much our daily thoughts impact our lives. They take hold of our power, telling us who we are and what are and aren't capable of. We are the only ones that have the power to take action to erase pesky thoughts from inhibiting our success in life.

I have found that organizing thoughts by writing them down makes them more abstract. When you can visualize them on paper, it makes them concrete.

Write out a list of pros and cons, random thoughts that pop up, poetry, grocery lists, anything that comes to mind. All writing can be therapeutic and helps us to rediscover how our voice sounds, which radiates who. I challenge to find yourself again with the power of good old pen and paper.

Learning to Love Yourself Again

To rediscover yourself, you need to learn how to love yourself again for who you are, and all parts of yourself, including your flaws and everything you have endured. There are millions of places that offer up 'good advice' to practice self-love, but they never explain exactly how to do so.

Loving yourself is a vital piece of the puzzle when it comes to positive personal growth. It allows us to fulfill our dreams and create happy and healthy relationships with others too.

Care about yourself as much as you care about others

This sounds almost too simple, but many of us are not selfish enough when it comes to fulfilling our wants and needs. It is hard to remember that you are **not** selfish when it comes to caring about yourself and your wellbeing.

Showing yourself compassion shows those in your life that you are able to take care of yourself. No one can pour from an empty pot, which means you need to take care of yourself in order to take care of others in your life. Treat yourself the way you treat your best friend, with caring, concern, and gentleness, no matter what is happening in your life.

Maintain boundaries

Jot down a list of things you need emotionally, both what is important to you and what upsets you. The list can be made up of anything, from wanting sympathy to being celebrated, to being cared for, etc. Whatever is important to you, no matter how silly it sounds, **Write. It. Down.**

We can often find ourselves smack dab in the middle of the confusing conflict and wonder how we got there in the first place. We ask ourselves how we attracted this situation and the people in it with us. While you still need to take responsibility for your actions, it is also crucial to not fall into a pit of self-blame that can cause stress, but rather really look into what is occurring. Many people lack inner confidence and have no idea what they are worth. This lack can leave us living in a sum-zero equation; we are loved completely or become completely unlovable.

I have found from my psychological studies and personal experiences that there are two very simple questions to help anyone restore healthy boundaries in their life to live a dignified life:

What does this situation negatively represent about yourself? How are you tolerating situations and the behaviors of those around you reinforces your low-worth within you? Those in our lives are a mirror of our own biases, hopes, and fears. *"All anger stems from anger at the self."*

What is your worst fear about saying "no"? Have you ever been left with the thought of you are a bad person because someone's behavior has left you feeling guilty? Well, stop! Challenge that thought by thinking about other situations you have been through. When that happens, the thought that you are a "bad person" falls apart. What matters, in the end, is simple math: people will either *add* or *subtract* to your life.

So, what have you written? The things you write are what you should consider your personal boundaries. When someone ignores something on that list, you should consider it as them crossing boundaries that you have respectively set for yourself. Do not ignore how you feel if this happens, for they are there to tell you what is right from wrong.

Inform others about the boundaries you have set for yourself and be forthcoming with what you will and will not tolerate. When you are assertive with your boundaries, this plays an important part in building a positive self-esteem and allows you many opportunities to reinforce your beliefs, what you cherish, and what you deserve from life.

Do YOU?

Take the time for yourself to establish the things that make you feel good about yourself and about your life as a whole, no matter what it is. Just learn to be aware of how you feel when you go about acting on certain things. For example:

- Are you exhausted by the work you do, but feel thrilled when gardening?
- Are you joyful when reading out loud to your children?
- Do you feel a sense of fulfillment when you write poetry or volunteer in your community?

Once you figure out what makes you feel good about yourself, make those things a priority by implementing them into your every day or weekly schedule. No matter what makes sure you go out and do them! This may mean you have to give up other things to make time for them, but it also means that you may need to re-evaluate your schedule and life more so that you are doing what you honestly enjoy.

To ensure that you are doing these things, there are more than likely going to have to be actions you take to get to those happiness goals, such as saving money to buy supplies to paint, waking up an hour earlier, exercising more, etc.

It is important to realize that you need to do what you need to in order to fulfill your happiness goals. You cannot allow yourself to blame others if you do not fulfill these things. It is time to be a little selfish and fill up your own teapot so that you can fill up the cups of others in your life! This will help you to not only feel better and do better by other people, but it will help you to clear the fog on inconsistent negativity from your life and enable you to truly love yourself and your life once more.